Psalms
OF A WOUNDED VESSEL

Psalms

OF A WOUNDED VESSEL

A BOOK OF POEMS AND INSPIRATIONAL READINGS

LAMESHIA SHAW-TANIMOWO

authorHOUSE®

AuthorHouse™
1663 Liberty Drive
Bloomington, IN 47403
www.authorhouse.com
Phone: 1-800-839-8640

Email requests to: so.melodic@yahoo.com

Unless otherwise notated, all scripture quotations are from the NKJV of the Bible

Any use of the NKJV text must include proper acknowledgement as follows:

Scripture taken from the New King James Version.
Copyright © 1979, 1980, 1982 by Thomas Nelson, Inc.
Used by permission. All rights reserved.

Definitions were used from . . . .

Encarta ® World English Dictionary © & (P) 1998-2004 Microsoft Corporation. All rights reserved.

Dictionary.com Unabridged (v 1.1)
Based on the Random House Unabridged Dictionary, Random House, Inc. 2006.

Online Etymology Dictionary, 2001 Douglas Harper

Published by AuthorHouse   07/03/2012

ISBN: 978-1-4520-1569-9 (sc)
ISBN: 978-1-4772-2880-7 (e)

Library of Congress Control Number: 2012911440

This book is printed on acid-free paper.

Contents

Dedication

This book is dedicated to my parents Faith McGill-Ivy and Andre Shaw. A special dedication is given in loving memory of my guardian angels Arthur R. Jones Sr., Jacqueline Newton, Shirley Ann White, Matthew Donahue and Daryl Keith Garrett.

Acknowledgements

JESUS - YOU ARE THE REASON FOR EVERYTHING! I LOVE, HONOR, AND ADORE YOU. YOU ARE MY SOURCE. THANK YOU FOR ALL OF MY GIFTS TALENTS, AND ABILITIES. I OFFER THEM ALL BACK TO YOU AS MY WORSHIP, FOR WITHOUT YOU I AM NOTHING. THANK YOU FOR THE LOVE AND FAVOR YOU'VE BESTOWED UPON ME. I LIVE TO WORSHIP YOU MY FATHER, MY GOD, MY FRIEND, MY SAVIOR, MY KING! I THANK YOU.

So many people have made an impact on my life. Some of those people I haven't seen nor spoken to in years. However there was something said or done that touched my life forever, and helped groom me into the woman that I am today. Whether I've known you for years or we've just crossed paths, you supported me with your kind words or a hard nudge, and for that I am eternally grateful.

I would like to give a special thank you to my Mommy, the number one supporter of any and everything I have ever dreamed of doing Faith McGill-Ivy. You always encouraged me to chase after my dreams at all cost and to keep God first. You showed me the real meaning of love, sacrifice, and consistency. I love, honor, and cherish you for being the best mother God ever crafted. You have always been my number one inspiration in all I set out to accomplish. I live to bring God glory and to make you proud! Thank you so much for your love and unselfishness. Thank you for putting me and my siblings first and always making sure we lacked nothing. There are not enough words in all of the languages combined to describe the love and gratitude I have for you. I just wanted the whole world to know how blessed I really am, to my Dad Andre Shaw, We have a special bond that not even the devil can break. We often laugh about how many things we have in common, but it is those things that I admire about you most! I am grateful that you are a part of my life. I love you more than words can express, and I'm starting to understand that no matter how old I get I will always be your baby girl, and I'm cool with that (smile). To my husband, Olumide Tanimowo, I get teary eyed just thinking about how blessed I am to have you in my life. How I must truly be favored by God for him to create such a special, loving, handsome, intelligent God fearing man just for me! You have treated me like a queen since the first day we met. Your love for me has never changed. Thank you for being my everything! Your titles changed a lot throughout this book writing process. You were my personal assistant, my editor, my errand runner, my manager and so much more but you never stopped being my husband and friend. Thank you for your love and support. I love you baby! To my grandparents; Rosetta McGill & James (Minnie) McGill, Millie Shaw & Dennis (Willa) Shaw. Your strength and sacrifice is the reason I can even follow my dreams today. I may get in trouble for this but I must say I don't think anyone could love you more than I do. To my siblings AJ Jones Jr., Patience Ivy, and LaTrisha Ivy, Wow what can I say? I love you all so much with the deepest love I know. I hope

that I was as great of a "big sister" as I think I was ha ha!
You all have been my babies since day one. The bond that
we have is so pure and genuine that no one will ever be
able to reproduce it or ever take your place in my heart.
You are my everything I love you and I am so proud of
each one of you. I know you have so much in you that I
can't wait 'til God pours it out of you. Know that the love
that I have for you runs wider than any ocean and that
my heartbeats only because you are in it. I love you three,
but I still will whoop you ha ah ha! Conquer the world
one dream at a time and every time you look behind you
or to your side, you will always find me there. To my Step
brothers and sisters Christopher Ivy Sr., Pastor Cynthia
Wolford, Vircy Carter, and Roman Douglas I love you
all so much I am so blessed to have you be a part of my
life. When our lives blended you loved me like we were
blood and became the big sisters and brothers I never
had. You imparted life into me and supported me in ways
some people pray their blood families would, thank you.
To my God sisters and God brother Dawn, Kayla and
Donald Muldrow, I love you always and forever. To my
nieces Centoria and Artaja and my nephew AJ, Jones
III, your existence brings me so much joy. I love and
miss you guys so much. You will grow up and do great
things because there is greatness inside of you. To my
God Mom Michelle Mills (who will probably kill me for
putting her name in the book, yet it's a risk I am willing
to take ha ah ha!) To some it all up you are just awesome!
You don't let me pout, you didn't allow me to give up
and you are dependable. You never tried to replace the
awesome mother I already have you just accompanied
her. You have been my shoulder to cry on, lean on, pray
on, complain on, and yet you never were afraid to keep

it real and stay on my case. When I needed someone the most and I was too far from home, you were there and I can never repay you for that. Your heart is as big as the earth we live on. Thanks for including me in it, I love me some you! To all of my nieces, nephews, aunts, uncles, cousins, other step brothers and sisters(Shawn, Tracy, Arietha, Latrice, Lil Arthur, Lisa and Shyra), friends and church family, you are my joy. Extra special thanks to my cousin-friends; Hope Garrett, Porsche Harris, Antoinette Richardson, and Shena Dreyfus, I love yal so much, smooches! To La Tonya Ford, Bianca Jones, Kenya Bates, LaKendra Tellis, Ursula Scruggs, Candice Jones, Barbara Kelley, Wendy Ivy, New Day Christian Church in Wichita Kansas, Dontae Walker, Tyrice Lollis, Raymond Lewis, Adrienne Silver, Iman Earsery, Jamellia Roddy, Thai Robinson, Andrae & LaKisha Kelley, Marquetta Kelley, Tammy Parker, Reginald Bell, Barbara Calderon, Marvella Townes, and Nicole Chavez, thanks for your love and friendship over the years. To the best pastors and spiritual parents on this side of heaven, Pastor Sammy & Co—Pastor Tracy James, & Destiny Worship Center in Augusta Georgia. You made sure that you pulled on every gift I have and you loved me as if I were your own. When I was broken you spoke life back into me. You two are amazing! Your hearts are pure and your love for God's people is truly priority one. May God bless you richly for being such a gift in my life, I love you. To Sylvia Franklin—Bryant, Pastor Moses & Doris Brown, Rev. Charles & Gaye Calhoun, Pastor Dearlin & Shatona Brown, and Pastor Fred & Tammie Hayes, you will always hold a special place in my heart. You all were my first pastors; youth leaders, choir directors, and mentors. You taught me the Word, how to love, how to praise, how to worship, and how to use my gifts for God's glory. You took me under your wings and helped cultivate my gifts, you opened up so many doors for me, and I will never forget it. This is the result of the seeds you have sown . . . it was in good soil and I just wanted to say thank you! To Shaneese Peek & the Book Worm Royalty Book Club, I love you ladies! To M&M Productions & my new family the cast of "Give it to God," stage play I love you all and I am so excited about what God is doing. Thank you for all of your love and support. To those I did not name you are no less important, and I thank you from the bottom of my heart for the love, wisdom, and guidance you have given me. I love you all.

LaMeshia "So Melodic" Shaw-Tanimowo

Definitions

Psalm

Sacred song or poem of praise: a sacred song or poem of praise, especially one in the Book of Psalms in the Bible [12th century. Via late Latin psalmus from Greek psalmos "harpsong," from psallein "to pluck."]

Wounded

1. injury to body: an injury in which the skin, tissue, or an organ is broken by some external force, for example, a blow or surgical incision, with damage to the underlying tissue

2. emotional injury: a lasting emotional or psychological injury still recovering from the wounds of a bitter divorce

3. injure: to cause a wound in the body of somebody or something, especially using a knife, gun, or other weapon He was wounded in the leg.

4. cause emotional wound: to cause somebody emotional or psychological distress by saying or doing something cutting remarks intended to wound

Vessel

A hollow or concave utensil, as a cup, bowl, pitcher, or vase, used for holding liquids or other contents.

Psalmist

writer of psalms: the author of a psalm

Lyricists

1. music songwriter: somebody who writes words for songs, especially popular songs. Also called lyrist
2. poetry lyric poet: a writer of lyric poems

Poet

1. poetry somebody who writes poems: somebody who writes poems, especially a regular and recognized writer of poems

2. somebody imaginative or creative: somebody who is very imaginative and creative or who possesses great skill and artistry and is able to produce beautiful things [13th century. Via French poète and Latin poeta from Greek poiētēs "maker, author," from poiein "to make."]

Introduction

"Psalms of a Wounded Vessel" is a compilation of poems, inspirational readings, songs, and quotes of my random thoughts and opinions. This book exposes the true feelings I had as I experienced different trials in my life. There was so much going on around me. I had my share of pain in many forms; I had been betrayed by people I loved and trusted, robbed at gunpoint, lost loved ones, financially challenged, depressed, discouraged, disappointed, rejected, neglected, overlooked, underappreciated, and the list goes on and on. Yes, I had been injured in this war called life. I had been *wounded* in battle and I could feel its sting. At times I was ready to give up, although I knew it was never an option. With the help of God I was able to make it through these difficult times. Writing is one of the ways that I expressed my pain, my outlook on life, the people and the things I love, my victories, as well as my dreams and my aspirations. These *Psalms* helped me put things back into perspective, and assisted me in overcoming the situations and disappointments that had caused me pain. Though this journey was not easy and this was a hard battle to fight, I am victorious! God transformed the battlefields of my pain into beautiful vineyards and playgrounds in my future. What was sent to destroy me instead designed me into who I am today. The good news is that wounds heal over time. I hope this book serves as an emergency first aid kit, that helps heal the *wounded* areas in your life. May you find love, laughter, strength and encouragement in these pages!

LaMeshia *"So Melodic"* Shaw—Tanimowo

~POEMS~

The Poet in Me

The poet in me makes my words dance across the page
Like MC Hammer every time he takes the stage
I want my words to remove your minds gloom
The way a candle illuminates a dark room

The poet in me, allows me to say things, some are afraid to mention
Using descriptive words and anecdotes to grab your attention
But, I want to be more than just rhymes, lines, quotes, and notes
Your inner most thoughts and feelings I want to provoke

The poet in me, permits me to control my environment, over words I have dominion
What I say is not always factual, most of it is just my opinion
I may not know the correct way to lay it out, of its techniques I was never trained
All I know is that I have to release theses thoughts, so that my mind is not drained

Yes the poet in me dwells deep inside
I can be in the middle of a conversation or see something move, and there goes my mind
Everything around me is intriguing, this is like my sixth sense
The poet is definitely a part of me, my writing is the evidence

A benefit of being a poet, is I get to see things, your mind can't began to conceive
So please forgive me if I blurt things out, or say things you do not believe
The beauty of being a poet is that every word is powerful
I feel like I am Ali and words are my punches, another round then its TKO

Lyricists, a writer, a rhymester, a psalmist, are a few other names for this disease
One that I desire no cure for, something I can handle with ease
As I share my thoughts with you, I'm sure I'll say something to which you do not agree
Again I ask you to forgive me, if I offend you, and blame it on the poet in me

FAMILY

1ST

Family

Dedicated to the Garrett-McGill, Dunford-Shaw Families

Our tree roots run deep, unmovable
Our features are as strong as our backbone
One simple glance and one can tell to whom we belong
Fighters until the end, "go getters" by all means
Beautiful in spirit and in stature, it's in our genes

Numerous disagreements, some mistreatments
Yet our laughter and love carries us through it all
From births to deaths, confusion to reunions
Special occasions to just because celebrations
We know how to get along

More than just a name, or playing card and board games
From PCP to the PHD and everything in between I love
you all the same
From black eyes to a bloody nose, Family photos and
talents shows
Yes this bond is unbreakable

Some of the most talented people I know
Not full of yourself, yet always the star of the show
Doing and saying things even Ripley's wouldn't believe
From creating a new word to a new hair weave

Yes we are the true definition of a functionally dysfunctional team
But we are easy to love, and if the truth be told, we have what others just dream
You are educated, funny, loving, and real
We share our love in different ways from hugs and kisses, from the kitchen to the grill

The legacy we will leave is far from counterfeit
The original no credit required lifetime membership
There is no social group that can take your place
You are my inner circle, connected by blood, kept by God's grace

Know that everything I do is for "we" not just for "me"
A writer, a poet, a singer, an actress, and entrepreneur
High school graduate, recipient of a college degree
Yet none of these accolades compare to the joy of having you as my family

I love you all!

My Special Place

Such a small box I'm in, yet I feel so free
It doesn't seem like a lot but everything I need is
surrounding me
The air is clean and clear, and I feel at my best
In here I can't remember my worries and troubles, my
heart is at rest

I'm in this place where everything seems so relaxed
A place where I can let it all go, and dream to the max
My inner thoughts and emotions I release when I am here
This place brings out the best in me, and blocks out all
my fear

In this place I can stay, for hours at a time
I can move and speak freely that which is on my mind
I come here often yet it never gets old
The temperature is just right, not too hot and not too
cold

Everything I ever desired is in arms reach or at least seems
to be
It's as if this place was created especially for me
But in this place, many people come and many people go
Yet everyone's experience is unique, a duplicate will never
show

Being here can be exhausting even though I am here to
unwind
I have to move quickly because I am being timed
Lay this here and lay that there
Move this here and move that there

I am on the clock but it doesn't feel that way
'Cause here I can do what I want, and say what I want
to say
Yes it is hard work and no it is not free
But I keep coming back because this is where I love to be

The time I spend here is amazing I never want it to end
Even before I leave I'm wondering when I can return
again
I'm always so full yet meals they never serve
Yet I am satisfied with my portion, I get what I deserve

This is such a fun and beautiful place to be
Though there is one thing to do and nothing much to see
So where is this place? I know you're dying to know
Well it's probably not what you were thinking, it's just the
studio.

I Just Wanna Sing

I don't need the fancy dress with sequence and all the rest
As long as when I open my mouth I do my best
I just wanna sing

You can keep your selfish attitudes and bad moods
Forgetting where you come from once you made it through
I just wanna sing

Just give me a mic' so I can feel that spark and the rest is history
It's how I release that which was deposited within me, my destiny
I just wanna sing

I don't have to have the interviews or be featured on the six o clock news
Don't need reporters and paparazzi digging through my personal issues
I just wanna sing

Winning a Grammy would be nice, but if not I'll be alright
As long as they don't take my voice away
I would love to have a cd and have a video on TV
As long as from my purpose I do not stray
I just wanna sing

My voice is my communication, my passport to other nations
It's my motivation, my inspiration, and my-self medication
I gotta sing

Singing is my gasoline, you see it keeps me going
It's the gift that God gave to me, so I gotta use it, I owe him
Just let me sing

As long as I can express myself in a melodic tone
I'll leave you and the rest of the world alone
I just wanna sing

You can keep your stage and the center page from the most popular magazine
Because this, is above all else I have ever dreamed
I just wanna sing

Predestined

Inspired by the preaching of Bishop Jim Dutton

I refuse to let my yesterday determine my tomorrow
I refuse to get comfortable dwelling in sorrow
I will no longer allow hurt and pain
For I have the right, to choose who will reign
I do not have to allow abuse, and stress
For if I hold on I am sure I can pass this test
No longer will I wallow in guilt in shame
But always call upon Jesus' name
I will not allow the enemy any space
But I will continue to read my word, fast, pray, and seek God's face
No man can tell me my beginning nor my end
For the word of God tells me it's already been written I am God's predestined.

Every dream, every goal that I have set out to attain
Has already been accomplished and stamped "Approved" in Jesus name
I can have, be, and do anything I ever desired to be
Because God said in His word that "I can do All Things through Christ who strengthens me."
A doctor, a lawyer, a teacher, a singer or a reverend
The way has already been made I am God's predestined

God knows that I will stumble, he has already factored in that I may fall

But just because I mess up doesn't mean that I'm not called

On my journey I've met pain, discouragement and despair

But I will get to where I am going because God says I'm already there

They are just road blocks set up to turn me around

But I am determined to reach my destiny, my purpose, my crown

So I will continue to push forward, my suggestion is that you do the same.

For I am a child of God and predestined is my name

Wounded

I am sure I am not the only one who has experienced tragedy. It comes in all forms, sizes and seasons. Maybe it was the loss of a loved one, the betrayal of a close friend or family member, being wrongfully accused, physically or emotionally abused, raped, molested, abandoned, mistreated, neglected, the victim of a crime or national disaster, so on and so forth. These experiences can leave wounds, or fragments of an unhealed situation. Often times these items are left unhealed because we shut ourselves down and no longer allow ourselves to trust, or even show our true sentiment. We become cocoons, sheltering our true emotions to avoid future hurt. We do not have to submit ourselves to devastation and despair. We can be set free. The Bible tells us in Isaiah 53:5b that *"By His stripes we are healed."* Not we can be, but we are healed. That is a declaration it has already been done. Once we believe that, these tragic experiences become memories of our past instead of mountains in our present.

I can remember an occasion when I wore a short-sleeved shirt and a kid in my youth group asked me, what happen to your arm? As I looked down at my arm, I could see him pointing at one of my scars. Then I remembered how I got it, and so I told him the story of how it all happened. The memory of the event was still there but my arm did not hurt anymore. It had been healed, the wound had closed and I only thought about again when someone else brought it up! That is how we have to look at our past hurtful situations. Once we have given them to God and he has healed them, all that is left is a scar, a memory. We remember when we were lied on, abused, talked about, and overlooked, but it does not hurt anymore, because we have released it to God. Look at your body. Look over your arms and your legs, what do you see? Look at the scars that life has left you. Search into your heart and see the scar tissues and the open wounds that are there. Today is your day of complete freedom! Release those past hurts, that unforgiveness, and those current situations to God. Pray and thank Him for the healing He said was already yours in Isaiah. Yes, you too were wounded by life but it did not break or destroy you. There is power in your testimony. Everything you have endured was for His glory. There is too much life still in you for you to allow the wounds to infect your gifts talents and dreams with the toxins and puss it holds. Let it go, now is the time for you to walk in your victory, look at yourself and see yourself healed!

Heaven Called Your Name

In Loving Memory of Shirley Ann White

The time has come, and we have to say goodbye
So today we sit in silence as we reminisce and cry
We do not understand exactly why you had to go
But we will never forget the love and kindness
That you were not ashamed to show

God knew exactly where you needed to be
So He called you home, away from all of your pain and
misery
Although this is very hard for us to face
We cannot be selfish, for we know you are in a better place
While you are away can you do a favor for me?
Please be a guardian angel and watch over our family
For this pain is almost too much for us to bear
So we need you to watch over us and remind us that you
are there

Say hello to Aunt Jackie and the rest of our family
And we promise that we will forever caress your memory
Jesus knew that you could no longer endure
So God said, Shirley, I will take away your pain
That was the day Heaven called your name

Who Are You?

Who are you discouragement, to tell me I can't make it
What gives you the right to beat me down until I just can't
take it?
How did you get in depression, how did you get me down
Who gave you permission to turn my whole world around?

Who are you deceit, to creep in with your lies and try to
make a mockery out of me
Why does your tongue speak against my character and say
things that your eyes did not see
You've got your nerve discontent, to come in and swallow
up my happiness
Remove my joys and my gratefulness and replaced them
with sadness

No more of you o lack of confidence, persuading me
against accepting who God created me to be
Goodbye debt, I am sick of being broke, I want those
things that God has promised me
I'm sure you can understand, abundance is what was
designed for me since the beginning of eternity

Now I speak to those things in my life that are not of God,
and demand them to flee
I will no longer be bound by theses chains, loose me now,
set me free
You have no right, no power no authority here, now nor
forevermore
Back to the pits of hell I command you to go, to return or
resurface in my life no more

For God has given me the power to cancel the works of
the enemy
So discouragement, depression, deceit, discontent, lack of
confidence and debt has to cease.
So I speak now, loud and bold like the clashing of two
large cymbals
Casting you out, calling on the name of Jesus which makes
every demon tremble.

Get out! Get out! You are not welcome here! I am more
than a conqueror, the Lord is my light and my salvation
whom shall I fear.
I know who you are and I've called you by name, I have
cast you out and the victory I will proclaim.
No longer will I cry, moan and groan and be mistreated
Because I know who you are. You are the enemy, the
serpent, the defeated.

Everything Happens for a Reason

You slipped in like a thief in the night but in broad
daylight
You were a coward so you tried to cover your face
You thought you had it all figured out and that your
arrest would never be
But you slipped on a few things and your features I
embedded into my memory
Everything Happens for a Reason
Contrary to popular belief it was neither because of
anything I said nor anything I did, that caused you to
place your gun to my face
No I didn't offend anyone in such a way that God was
paying me back. This was not revenge, for you and I have
never met
Everything Happens for a Reason
Was there a great lesson to be learned from this tragic
event?
Perhaps I was just the vessel God chose to show others
that He will remain faithful even when the adversary
plans to take you out.
Everything Happens for a Reason
See He covered me and that is what I rejoice in.
I sustained no physical injuries, and your gun never
went off
I realize it could have been much worse but I was being
protected by my creator so that I could be a living
testimony of the strength that He posses

Everything Happens for a Reason

With the eyes of the enemy himself you looked at me and demanded I give you money
Yet that which is most valuable to me you could not take
My salvation and my joy are eternal
Even if you had stolen my last breath they would have still remained

Everything Happens for a Reason

For five hundred and sixty some odd dollars and some change
You bought you a fully furnished jail cell equipped with everything you need to waste your life away and I am certain that when you are finally sentenced justice will be served

Everything Happens for a Reason

No my life will never be the same yet I've learned so much through this
Yes I forgive the both of you and I pray you find salvation before judgment day
That morning, I will never forget but glory to God, neither will you

Everything Happens for a Reason

My prayer is that you understand that you changed my life, yours and that of our families the day you allowed Satan to use you. Repent and receive the salvation of the Lord is what I am asking of you, yes more than your jail time. O how I wish you would've known that you didn't need to rob me, God would have provided for you if you would have allowed him.

Everything Happens for a Reason

These are just some of the things that were on my mind
although I rarely rhymed
Thanking my heavenly father in and out of season
Because now I truly understand that everything happens
for a reason

Without You

In Loving Memory of Arthur R. Jones Sr.

I reach for you, yet I am unable to touch you
I call for you and there is no answer
I cry for you yet there is no response
I can't believe this is actually happening
I don't wanna be without you

Time has no restrictions, no one can pinpoint when it began or when it will end
Life was given no time stamp, no real peak into its system of departure
Life has only one certainty, just as sure as you live, you shall die

I reach for you, yet I am unable to touch you
I call for you and there is no answer
I cry for you yet there is no response
I can't believe this is actually happening
I don't wanna be without you

I knew you could not live forever but I wish you were still here
So many things you didn't get a chance to see me accomplish, that thought brings me to tears
No regrets have I, for our relationship was good
Our love for one another though not always spoken was definitely understood
My baby brother and I will always cherish your memory
There is one thing that cannot be contested—we were a family

I love you more than you will ever know
Being without you is like experiencing a blizzard without the snow
I honor and respect you in so many ways
Being without you is like the sun without its rays
Such an impact you have made on my life
Being without you is like being pierced in the heart with a knife
Many people missed out on the real you
They were too busy focusing on what they think you did or did not do
They didn't give you a chance to show your love and affection
They really missed the mark—having you in my life was such a blessin'

Gone but not forgotten
I loved you then and I love you now
Contrary to popular belief you were a good man
A great father to those who gave you a chance
A great friend, brother, uncle, and definitely a working man
Such a giver you were, I will always hold you near to my heart
The reason I do not want to stop writing this poem—also the reason for its start

I reach for you, yet I am unable to touch you
I call for you and there is no answer
I cry for you yet there is no response
I can't believe this is actually happening
I don't wanna be without you

I love you so much, and I hate to see you go
You won't be around to watch your grandchildren grow
You taught me how to love everyone despite their faults
How to forgive those who hurt me with their lies and evil thoughts
You encouraged me to chase my dreams, and how not to consider that I may fall
I will always be your little "buzzard", your "baby", your "meatball."
How I wish this was all a dream and you would return and I could see your face
But I don't want to be selfish—I know you are in a better place

I wish I could have one more hug, one more kiss
I wish when I called for you, my call you did not miss
I wish that as I cried you'd come and wipe my tears away
I wish that we could hang out and love on one another,
just one more day

But . . .
I reach for you, yet I am unable to touch you
I call for you and there is no answer
I cry for you yet there is no response
I can't believe this is actually happening
I don't wanna be without you
I love you—I miss you

Tongue Lashers Anthem

Blah, blah, blah, blah, blah
You can't stop me, no matter how hard you try
No, no, no, no way
Will you triumph over me another day
Get, get, get, get back
For I know how to really fight when I am under attack
Everything I set out to do, will get done
If I were you, I'd watch my tongue

Funny how you open your mouths when it should be closed
Close your mouth when it should be open, and toot up your nose
Liars, gossipers, haters, many names I've heard you called
Your purpose I am sure of, but at some of your behaviors I am appalled

You allow your imagination to run untamed, and your lies you spread with a loud shout
Making up things about me, and repeating things you know absolutely nothing about
Do you really have a reason to dislike me?
Or is it because I had the courage to chase after my dreams

Blah, blah, blah, blah, blah
You can't stop me, no matter how hard you try
No, no, no, no way
Will you triumph over me another day
Get, get, get, get back
For I know how to really fight when I am under attack
Everything I set out to do, will get done
If I were you, I'd watch my tongue

I know my persistence simply ticks you off
The way I carry myself despite your attempts to destroy
me at all cost
Aggravated because the stumbling blocks you set up, I
always seem to get around
And though sometime you scratch my last nerve I never
hit the ground

Extra! Extra! I have great news for you
Come up with some new schemes is what I encourage you
to do
I'll always have something for you to talk about, my dreams
are in high demand
So as long as you are in the hating business, in the
unemployment line you will never stand

Blah, blah, blah, blah, blah
You can't stop me, no matter how hard you try
No, no, no, no way
Will you triumph over me another day
Get, get, get, get back
For I know how to really fight when I am under attack
Everything I set out to do, will get done
If I were you, I'd watch my tongue

Don't be confused honey I wrote this one especially for you
Truth be told you were my motivation, you helped push
me through
I know, I know this was not your intention
But I control my destiny, and I set its dimensions

What I'm simply saying is that you are wasting your time
Keep spreading your lies, and rollin' ya eyes. I've got bigger
things in mind
Because the more you push the more I'll press
I do my best when you spread your mess

Blah, blah, blah, blah, blah
You can't stop me, no matter how hard you try
No, no, no, no way
Will you triumph over me another day
Get, get, get, get back
For I know how to really fight when I am under attack
Everything I set out to do, will get done
If I were you, I'd watch my tongue

Blah, blah, blah, blah, blah
You can't stop me, no matter how hard you try
Everything I set out to do, will get done
If I were you, I'd watch my tongue

A Time for Change

"If I am going to do the same thing today, that I did yesterday, what is the purpose for tomorrow? Because soon tomorrow will be today, and today will be yesterday, and I would have spent them all the same."
LaMeshia "So Melodic" Tanimowo

Can you imagine living the same day over and over for the rest of your life? It would defeat the purpose of life itself, because you would do the same thing day in and day out and the results would be the same at the end of the day. You would not be anxious for tomorrow, because it will be lived the same as yesterday and today. What a waste of God's gift to us, the gift of life.

It sounds inconceivable doesn't it? How can you actually live the same day over and over? Well we may not ever see the same calendar date again, but often times our actions and reactions have us spinning in a whirlwind of familiarities. We do things repetitiously and expect a different outcome from the one before, although we refuse to change anything in the original equation. How can we say that we are sick of our situation, and not be willing to change our lifestyle in such a way that it can sustain the change we say we are in need of? We have to understand that in order for our situation to change we have to modify something in our life.

Often times we host a lavish pity party for ourselves. Decorated with excuses, of why our dreams we have not fulfilled. There, we serve an exquisite entrée of lies, doubt, and yes even fear. Some of us even have the audacity to invite others to our pity party, and others of us use a theme called our past, to give vivid examples of why we could never be where we dream of being. Boo hoo! Get over yourself, and get on the move! Yes we have all experienced things in our life that detoured us on our journey to our destiny. However it is up to you alone, whether you allow those situations to pause or paralyze you.

That business you want to start, that new invention, that song you are to write, you overlook and make every excuse for because you are secretly afraid of failure and change. True dreamers and visionaries embrace change, because they realize that in order to go to the next level, they will have to give up something or someone to get to where they need to be. It requires us to step out of our comfort zone.

If you really want something extraordinary to happen in your life, you will have to do something extraordinary. By that I mean something that differs from your norm, do something unusual. You must take sensible steps to your goal. I'm sure if we ask any pro athlete to name one of the things they had to do to achieve their dream; one of the answers that would repeat itself would be training and conditioning their bodies. You cannot even plan to make the team sitting on the couch. The same is true for your personal goals. There must be a conditioning of your mind, a training of new skills. The saying "you can be anything you desire to be," is more than just a popular cliché. Your success lies in your hands and if you dare to be an achiever you must first embrace change and secondly control the atmosphere with your actions.

Life is one of God's most precious gifts to us. If we are going to be here we may as well live life to the fullest. And you will never walk in abundance until you fully walk into your destiny. I say that because no matter how good it looks on the outside, you will always feel as if something is missing. It is a void your money will not be able to fill, a wound that Neosporin will be unable to heal. Look around, change is happening all around you. Despite your resistance and the gnashing or your teeth, you will be unable to stop the world from changing. However, you have the choice to stop being the victim of your past or even your current situation. Some of the most successful people have horror stories of what it took to get them to where they are today.

What are you willing to let go of to get to where you need to be? What are you ready to do? Will you enroll in school, train and condition your body, pull that secret box, full of your ideas and projects out and began working on them again? How will you handle this change? Will you continue to run from it and be left behind? Or are you finally ready to say yes to yourself? You've been saying yes to others for so long. You've been the number one supporter of those near you, but can you handle the pressure that comes along with supporting you? Are you even willing to try, or when the new year hits, will you look back on the previous year and see that you keep your same score, dreams—0, excuses 5?

Whatever you decide to do, make sure it is beneficial to where you really want to go. Change isn't as scary as you think. When you finally get there, you will be asking yourself what took you so long. Do a self inventory and make changes accordingly. No one knows what you need and desire more than you!

W.O.W.

(Wonders of His Works)

Have you ever had a moment in your life when you just looked around and were amazed? Have you ever stood outside and looked at the beauty of creation? Glancing over the fields and noticing that no two trees are the same, or that every flower has its own unique scent? Have you ever taken the time to think about how many different species of animals there are, or why they all have an appetite for something different?

Have you ever noticed the sound that the wind makes as it blows by you, though it's face you never see? Have you considered the strength of the ground we walk on, to be able to sustain after earthquakes, tornadoes, floods, fires, asteroids, vicious hurricanes and lighting? Isn't it amazing how the seasons always end and begin at its respective times, year after year?

Have you noticed how the clouds, the stars, the moon, and the sun, hang high in the sky day by day and never fall down? Or how the oceans, rivers, lakes and the seas stay in place never overtaking the ground? What a site to see the mountains stand tall and the beauty of its peak? Or how the hills add definition to the earth as the deserts and valleys lye low and yet still speak.

Have you ever looked out the window and watched the falling of the rain or snow? Did you notice that every drop and every flake knew exactly where to go? Have you ever looked around and said wow, life is amazing. How could this be? Have you taken the time to listen to the evolution theory?

It puzzles me how something they say blew together recreates and reproduces. How from an explosion everything and everyone has its own DNA and fingerprint, and each fruit gives off different juices. I'm not here to point fingers or say that they are wrong. I just want to expose the truth, nature has been saying all along.

Maybe they are right. What if the bang that they speak of, were the echoes of God's voice as He said "let there be." Maybe it's nothing at all, maybe it's just me. Call me crazy, blind or what you will, it doesn't hurt. Because every time I look around I say wow, wow, wow. W.O.W. WOW I see the **W**onders **O**f His **W**orks.

Now

Hello God, I know that you have a lot of people calling
on you today
But it is I, your servant, and I need you to make a way
Everything around me seems to be going wrong
I can't seem to attain my finances, my praise, my song

Chaos has become my shelter and frustration my
roommate
And it seems that anxiety and despair have become innate
You said, whenever I need you, all I have to do is call
I tried to do it on my own, I messed up, so down on my
knees I fall

I believe in your word, I believe it all to be true
So I am walking in "Now" faith just like the eleventh
chapter of Hebrews
I know, the renewing of strength comes to they that wait
But what I can't understand, is how long the process
actually takes

It seems that if I walk in now faith I should walk in now
blessings
The promise of prosperity, peace, abundant life, and love
gives my heart a little resting.
But Father it is not enough for me to know that they are
on the way
I need to reach out and touch them, for I am in need of
them today

King of kings, Lord of lords, Mighty One, please hear
my cry
I am reaching out to you like the woman with the issue of
blood, please do not pass me by
I wanna be the one you hear, like in John chapter nine
verse thirty-one
Or like the servants with the talents in Matthew
twenty-five, that heard servant well done

Abba, El Shaddai, Jireh, Ropha, Holy, Righteous, Worthy
Lamb
Burden Barer, Heavy Load Sharer, Prince of Peace, Rock
of Ages, the Great I Am
The question is not if? It's When? You are Jehovah Nissi,
so I know that you will make a way somehow
But I need you more than yesterday more than tomorrow
Lord I need you now

Man of My Dreams

A knight in shining armor, the one who holds the missing glass slipper
The man behind the mask the friend, the lover, the great kisser
The one who holds my hand as we stroll the beach at sunset
The one who makes my heart skip a beat, a man who follows God's foot steps

Mr. Romantic. Flowers, candy, cards, and vacations just because
A gentleman at all times, not ashamed to publicly expose his love
A joker, a kidder a man who makes me smile when I should cry
Yet serious, knows how to take care of business, and not afraid to try

Strong yet tender, wise yet approachable, confident yet humble
Opinionated yet a great listener, respected yet kind, educated so he doesn't mumble
Well put together from head to toe Mr. Debonair
Whenever he speaks people listen, whenever he walks they stare

Hands of a working man, however sheik in stature
My prince charming, my happily ever after
His touch as soft as a rose petal, his breath a sweet as can be
His lips as juicy as a melon surrounding his pearly white teeth.

His skin is flawless he has vigor in his bones
He is the definition of a real man, committed, honest, loyal, and strong
A provider, a lover, and a friend, the brotha's got it going on.

A praying a man, one who knows how to keep his house in order
A man who respects his father, his God, and honors his sisters and his mother
A man who knows what he wants and who he is, not a "down low brother"

A family man, he knows how to balance his time
He's like a scene from my favorite movie . . . Rewind
A protector by nature, like a super hero, he'd rescue me
And if I had a long day at work he'd help me with the dishes and rub my feet.

Everyone wishes they had one like you, your DNA is worth duplicating
But you are one of a kind, sent from heaven so they'll just be waiting
Indescribable is my attraction toward you.
I love the way you smell, the style of your hair, baby do what you do

You're not perfect by any means but not afraid to apologize
You are who you are, nothing else, you don't wear a disguise
You never put me down, communication is our guide
You never leave me behind, I'm always by your side

Its six o'clock in the morning, the alarm sounds I must begin another day
A slight rub on my shoulder, and I hear a voice say it's time to awake
I exhale deeply, angered because I don't want this to end.
I stretch my legs as I yawn making this moment last as long as I can
I open my eyes and to my surprise I'm greeted with a kiss from the softest pair of lips
I've ever felt.
As I sit on the side of my bed scratching my head, my heart began to melt

The man looking in my eyes looks so familiar to me.
He looks at me with confused eyes and says baby are you ok? How did you sleep?
A light scent of lavender fills the room, from my bath that he's already drawn
He kisses the top of my forehead and says breakfast is waiting we gotta get goin' come on

With a shaky voice "Good morning baby" I finally replied
I cannot believe what I am seeing, everything is jumping
on the inside
I arise singing a joyful song ready to conquer the world,
what a great day this will be
Because the man of my dreams, was more than a fairy tale.
He really belongs to me

From Chains to Change

Dark skinned—broad shoulders-hair of wool, strong
calves and arms of steel.
With the strength of a bear, the intelligence of a genius,
and the heart of a babe he was taken away in chains.
From the throne of his country to a ship full of his
brothers-, he was carried to a new land. They stripped
him from his family, changed his language and his name.
Swept away from his native land forced to work for "the
man" with his bare hands. Unable to read or write, he
never gave up his fight, beaten, battered and bruised
trying to protect his family
Cut down, sold, and mistreated, yet never lost his sanity.
Though malnourished his mind flourished and he was
somehow able to maintain a "yes I can" attitude.
Year's past—the same circumstances alas still he never
gave up the dream of being free once again.
Through cruel intentions, he created witty inventions
that changed the new nation.
The lights that gave it power, the food that fed it, the
material that clothed it, were just some of his creation.
His wife bore children unknown to him but the love for
his family and his God never diminished.
Planning and plotting in the still of the night, and
praying is what kept his soul replenished.

Through the swamps and hot fields, rivers, streams and the underground, he tread. Hungry, tired—barefoot and bleeding yet pressing full speed ahead.

Freed from slavery after decades of pain.

Confirmed by the emancipation proclamation that freedom was something he could gain. Not all peachy still bumpy roads to trod.

Unable to ride the front seat on a bus, vote, nor eat at a restaurant.

Signs reading white only filled his heart with pain, being segregated, and lynched for the color of his skin and the sound of his name.

Freed to be imprisoned by society, receiving unfair treatment based solely on his nationality.

Still pressing, still pushing he marched until his voice was heard. Declaring what he had "Dreamed," confirming it with God's Word.

He stood with a loud voice and a humble cry professing that this too shall pass. Strengthening the Faith of an entire nation, with the hope of being "Free at Last."

Educated business owners, inventors, surgeons, teachers, lawyers, preachers, athletes, singers, actors, congressmen, senators, governors, protectors of the country that we now adore.

Designers, mayors, builders, anchormen, doctors, directors, authors, poets, astronauts, comedians, and so much more.

What a long road to freedom, something to be happy for.

Such an honor and a privilege to go from "yes sa massa" to president number 44.

What an inspiration it is to live and see that which was once called impossible move to certainty.

To God I am thankful and to him I give all honor despite all the drama.

Because He showed himself faithful and moved His people from Kunta Kente to Barak Obama!

Love Defined

It's been said that love is patient love is kind
Love does not discriminate. Love is colorblind
Love is gentle love is sweet
Love never suffers the agony of defeat

Love is the absence of abuse the presence of support
It is more than a fancy ceremony more than standing
before a judge in court
Love is unconditional love is true
Love is getting to the root of the issue

Love does not cause harm love does not cause fear
Love is not measured by money or the relationship's
amount of years
Love can sustain the roughest times for love is secure
Love has no time restrictions, for any eternity it can
endure

Love understands love does not blame
Love is forgiving it doesn't house guilt or shame
It's been said that "God is love" and if that is true
Then love is the spirit of God dwelling inside of you

To truly love we must be as unselfish as God was, to give
His only son
We must be determined like Jesus still willing to go to the
cross though it was for nothing He had done
We must be as faithful as the Holy Spirit always there for
one another and a comfort to those in need
If we could do these few things, we could love indeed

It's been said that "God is love" and if that is true
Then love is the spirit of God dwelling inside of you
And where the spirit of the Lord is there is liberty
So live to love and love so that you may be free

Hephzibah

The History

1. **A Queen**—Hephzibah was the queen of Jerusalem/ Judah
   * The wife of King Hezekiah
   * The Mother of King Manasseh
   *** **Citation: 2 Kings 21:1** ***

2. Reference to Jerusalem denoting the prophesied restoration to the Jews after captivity

   *** **Citation:** Isaiah 62:4 and www.dictionary.com

Dictionary.com Unabridged (v 1.1)
Based on the Random House Unabridged Dictionary, ©
Random House, Inc. 2006.

The Story Pt. 1

In the fall of 2007 I relocated from Kansas to Georgia. There are many factors and reasons for this move. I was in a place in my life where I knew that I really wanted to get closer to God, and walk in my "Divine Purpose." I was born and raised in Kansas and I had a lot of family and church members there. I felt like I was ready to run this race. It was as if I had my running gear on, I had laced my shoes and I was at the starting line. But instead of everyone cheering me on, they indirectly held me back. There was a lot of resistance or a lot of . . . "In a few years that will be you" or" I can't wait 'til you are ready to do that." When the truth of the matter was that I was ready but somehow my past had fogged their vision and it was if I was the only one who could see my future. I did have some people around me who understood just what I needed, and that was a change. I had prayed to God asking for an answer. We had just started a gospel group and we wanted God to move in that situation as well. Condensing the story, the group had an opportunity to relocate to Georgia and everything fell in place. What an opportunity for me to start over around people who know nothing about me, and I can have the freedom to grow without opposition. We decided to move to Augusta, and so we did. Our manager, who is also my aunt, preceded us in this move. She found some nice apartments right outside of Augusta (see Pinnacle for part two of the story), in a little town called Hephzibah. My initial reaction was "Where?"

I thought oh man what a name, and we laughed and joked about it. Things started out great when I moved here and I had never felt better. Then things started to change as time progressed. I found myself asking God why He brought me here. He told me that this was the place for me and that it was my turn, and now everything was falling apart. Then I heard him say, research where you live. It took weeks for me to understand what He meant. I was doing all kinds of research on Georgia and Augusta and I could not understand what He meant. One day while I was praying he said "Literally!!" I thought uh ok, so I looked up the name of my apartment complex and it changed my attitude and I was so blessed. (Pinnacle). I was sure I had the answer, he did not tell me there was more to the story. So I began to walk around encouraged. A month later as I was studying my Bible, I came across 2 Kings 21:1. When it said Hephzibah I lost it. It didn't say much, but from the scripture I read I knew she was a queen. So I researched it and sure enough, she was a queen. WOW!!! This name I had been joking about all along had a biblical background. As I dug deeper into it I found that it also appears in Isaiah. How come I never heard of this woman? What I found out was so powerful and so refreshing combined with what I had already learned about the name of my complex, that I knew God was working this thing out. See to some people it may just be a coincidence, but I believe it was by "Divine Intervention." That God purposely set up "Divine Connections and "Divine Destinations" to help me reach my "Divine Purpose." Everything started to make complete sense. I don't know why I was looking up Augusta and never thought to look up Hephzibah. I was blown away. Tears filled my eyes and I was overjoyed at the revelation God had given to me, again during my personal quiet time with Him. When we first arrived in Georgia, I had an engagement to sing in a choir, behind Grammy Award Winner, Pastor Hezekiah Walker. Then a spot opened so my group could be one of the opening acts for the show. I am definitely a fan of his music. However, I did not know he could preach! Wow! I was so inspired. I still listen to the tape. He said so much that hit home. One thing he said really blessed me. Remember how I was saying I felt like I was at the starting line but I was being held back. He doesn't know it, but the revelation was for me. He said that there are people of your past, people of your present and people of your future. Now I had heard this preached before but never like this. The part that was for me was the people in my present. See the people of my past had released me. He said there are people in your present that are not supposed to be a part of your future and they know that. He went on to say those people "don't want to see you go backwards to your past, but don't want you to move forward to your future. Because they know that if you move forward into your future, they will become a thing of your past." O my! It made so much sense. That's why I had to move, yea I had people around me that loved me and wanted to see me do better, but the reason I was being held back was because they didn't want to become an object of my past. That was such a rich word for me, and it just so happened to past the lips of one of my favorite artist. The ironic part is that his name is Hezekiah! Yep, Hezekiah, Queen Hephzibah's King. Amazing how God works. Coincidence, ironic, whatever you want to call it. I received the words God had been trying to speak to me, when I reached Hephzibah.

The Definition

Hephzibah—

1. "My delight is in her" (God's delight) another word for Zion or God's Favor.

2. Proper biblical name, from the Hebrew language literally meaning "My Delight is in her." From the word *hephtzi*—"My delight" or to desire, and *bah*—meaning "in her"

Citation: *Online Etymology Dictionary,*
© *2001 Douglas Harper*

The Revelation

Isaiah 62:4-5
New International Version (NIV)
⁴ *No longer will they call you Deserted, or name your land Desolate.*
But you will be called Hephzibah,[a] *and your land Beulah*[b]*; for the Lord will take delight in you, and your land will be married.*
⁵ *As a young man marries a young woman, so will your Builder marry you;*
as a bridegroom rejoices over his bride so will your God rejoice over you.

Isaiah 62:1-12 (*4)—God says I have not forgotten about you. And He will not rest until righteousness goes forth. He will put you in a place where even those who counted you out will see you walking worthy. See you moving in your calling . . . your Divine Purpose! He is going to give you a new name. A name that will be from his mouth, not the names the world has given you. You will be a crown of Glory for the Lord (his mouthpiece, His trophy, His jewel) Allowing Him to use you for His glory. A royal power in his hand (bold spirit). You shall no longer be called abandoned and you will no longer lack anything. You shall be called "**Hephzibah.**"

For the Lord delights in you. And he rejoices over you. He has sent watchmen over you. So stand firm and speak what thus saith the Lord. Speak it until there is a change in the atmosphere and until there is a praise in the earth. This is the promise of the Lord; No longer will your enemies have triumph over you. This is your season, and you will reap your rewards. Everything you have labored over, every seed you have planted. You will eat!!! And God will be glorified. You will be in His presence. Go Forth and prepare the way for the people! Lift up the banner for the people! (Be an example. Be a living testimony.) For God says your breakthrough is coming. And all the rewards you have been waiting on. Because you are holy, redeemed of the Lord. You will be sought out and not forsaken! Be encouraged. Go Forth!

The Wait

Tick tock, tick tock

Another second has passed on the clock
Fifty-nine more of them will equal a minute
Sixty minutes, is as one hour, and twenty-four hours is as
one day

Tick tock, tick tock

So much to do but it seems I have so little time to do it
Have to do this—must do that
So many plans so many demands it seems as if time is
slipping through my fingers

Tick tock, tick tock

Time is moving fast but change is moving slow
Not really sure what should be by next move
Hmmm which way should I go?

Tick tock, tick tock

If I do nothing, I will surely get nothing
Time is precious not one moment can be repeated
I don't want to rush it, but I know I must get things done
before it's too late

Tick tock, Tick tock

For everything there is a time and a season
But if I take too long opportunity may pass me by
I've been told that good things come to those that wait

Tick tock, tick tock

There are seven days in one week
Four weeks in a month
And there are twelve months in a year

Tick tock, tick tock

Stop running your mouth, quit making excuses
Don't let time pass you by, get moving!
The wait is over!

Love Letter

Your smile is infectious, it releases a delightful glow
Your kiss is gentle, as soft as the freshly fallen snow
Your personality is uplifting, you always make me smile
Your conversation is intriguing, you keep my attention all
the while

Your scent is sweet, a lovely fragrance I cannot name
Your touch, as a healing oil, it wipes away all my pain
Just the mention of your name, makes my knees get weak
I can feel the tenderness of your breath upon me every
time you speak

You promise me the world, you say that the sky is the limit
And when you tell me you love me, I know you really
mean it
Loneliness has diminished to a mere whisper since you've
been here
No more hurting, no more sadness, no more emptiness,
no more tears

You're so attentive, when I talk I know you really listen
You're the perfect man for me, everything that I've been
missin'
When you're here, I am at peace because I know
everything is under control
You are my comforter, my best friend, you are Jesus, the
lover of my soul

My Angels

I'm calling on the angels who are assigned to me.
From the north, to the south, and the west to the east
I am dispatching them from the heavens high, to the earth
and in between
To bring me the things that has been promised to me

I send my financial angels all around
From the high skies to beneath the ground
To claim what is mine, and to bring it back to me
My inventions, my money and my creativity
I send them across the waters and the dry lands
To recover my stole blessings and to place them into my
hands

Go forth angels and recover my dreams, my hopes and my
career
Be swift and persistent for the end is drawing near
Venture out angels of wisdom and peace
Look high, low, far and wide, snatch back my mind and
my hearts release

Take flight angels, spread your wings and fly high
For the breathe of God is the wind that pushes you through
the sky
Your halo is the eye of God a ring of light that illuminates
the dark places
It will navigate you through the storms and calculate your
paces

Repossess all the things that were assigned to me,
Do not return to your mission is complete
From the east to the west from the south to the north
I am dispatching my dear angels, to go forth

Sifted

** *Chuek pronounced (chew-k)*

Chuek chuek chuek chuek chuek chuek chuek chuek chuek chuek
Well mannered and fun-loving is how my mom would describe me as a child
Creative, full of life, respectful, never wild
Beautiful and intelligent, a student of straight A's
Rarely chastised, I could be straightened with the "mother's gaze"

Chuek chuek chuek chuek chuek chuek chuek chuek chuek chuek
Adventurous to some degree, yet not a fan of trouble
A believer in family, always there when they need me on the double
A performer of many tasks, however always efficient
Easy to get along with, nevertheless always different

Chuek chuek chuek chuek chuek chuek chuek chuek chuek chuek
Quick to say "no" while everyone is saying "yes"
A leader fa' sho, with no tolerance for mess
Jail, drugs, and gangs, I never got a taste
Born with so many gifts and talents ready to be used, no need to go to waste

Chuek chuek chuek chuek chuek chuek chuek chuek chuek chuek

Couldn't go to the parties, at the time it seemed so unfair
Now I realize it was God was separating the wheat from the tare
When I was a child I thought as a child, as I grew older I came to understand,
That God had a plan for me, a purpose, my life was in His hands

Chuek chuek chuek chuek chuek chuek chuek chuek chuek chuek

Chosen-predestined-called—and justified by grace
Don't get it twisted I'm far from perfect, I still haven't seen His face
So many times I did wrong, even though I knew what was right
Yet He forgave me every time, and called me pleasing in His sight

Chuek chuek chuek chuek chuek chuek chuek chuek chuek chuek

Commissioned by His son to let the world know
That Heaven is a real place that He wants everyone to go
So He equipped me with destiny, and anointed me with plans

Chuek chuek chuek chuek chuek chuek chuek chuek chuek chuek
Chuek chuek chuek chuek chuek chuek chuek chuek chuek chuek
Is the sound I heard from Heaven
While I was being *sifted* in the Master's hands

Divine Purpose

(the Poem)

In the beginning you created the entire universe by saying
let there be
Yet you took the extra time and care and used your hands
when you created me
From the dust of the earth you molded man in your
image and gave him your very breath
Giving him dominion over every living creature, you
loved him, you made him flesh

You gave him a tour of the garden and showed him, off
which trees he could eat
And when you finished presenting Eden to him, you
caused him to fall asleep
As he slumbered, you took one of his ribs, sealed up his
wounds and designed me
You didn't speak it, you used your hands and the flesh of
man which lets me know I am special to thee.

Created in your image, and completed by your breath, is
what makes me divine
To you, I am a masterpiece, something that only you can
define.
The shape of my eyes, the fullness of my lips and hips, is
evidence that you took your time to make me unique.
The originality of personality, my voice, my laugh,
confirms your intelligence every time I speak.

You sent me out to the earth and assigned a purpose to me
Advising me that if I fail to utilize all my gifts and talents
I would never be all you created me to be
So I started out on the right path but I admit I went
astray
There were so many other things that were pleasing to my
eye that set my journey back a day.
I remember what you instructed me, and commanded me
off that tree I shall not eat
But the color of its fruit looked so beautiful and the taste
o so sweet.
But it was a trick how could one wrong turn cause so
much pain
Forgive me Father for I don't want the life I live to be in
vain

God help me to reach my destination, and while you're at
it help my brothers and sisters too.
Ok, ok Lord I hear you, o yea, that is what you sent me
out to do
I know you whispered the purpose of my life in my ear
A soft and gentle voice you spoke, but your words were
very clear

Go forth my daughter into all the nations
Live a life that reflects my creations
Sing songs of hope, speak words of wisdom
Write psalms of encouragement, dance to my rhythm

Go forth my sweet child don't forget the instructions I
have given you
For you are the only person that can complete this
assignment,
I have something else planned for Jimmy, something else
for Jane
If you fail to complete your assignment the world will
never be the same

Get up my child, back on your feet you go
You must finish this assignment so the rest of the world
will know
Know that I AM Alpha and Omega the beginning and
the End
That unless they come through me, in heaven they will
never get in

Get up daughter you can finish the race
I filled your life with destiny, purpose, love, and my grace
Stand up woman of God save those tears
My children are out there hurting and do not know I will
conquer all of their fears

Stand tall princess you are royalty
Don't let the burdens of this world get you down there is
a mission you must accomplish
Dust yourself off beautiful you will never be complete
until your purpose is fulfilled
I've given you everything you need to finish this thing.
It's been written in my will

Divine Purpose is what I've given you don't you
understand
If I have placed it inside of you, it can be taken by no man
Get up sing, write, teach, tell your story
Remember I said to use all those gifts, but use them for
my glory

Divine Purpose is the reason you are still here, it's the
push you feel
It is what keeps you connected to me, it reminds you that
I am real
I understand that times get rough and life seems hard to
bare
But I am always here for you, and I am here because I care

You have been given instructions my child, don't forget
obedience is important to me
For if you decide to throw in the towel chastisement you
will receive
I've forgiven you of your sins, and cast them away, do not
allow them to resurface
Go forth my child Go forth, and achieve your Divine
Purpose.

Pinnacle

The Story (Part 2)

When I first moved to Georgia, I moved into some apartments my aunt had found in Hephzibah. I arrived there and the apartments were nice, quiet and clean, just like I like them. The two ladies in the office were just adorable and sweet as can be. They were helpful and friendly, perhaps my very first taste of southern hospitality. My neighbors were so funny! Everyone in my building was really cool. The apartment directly across from me was empty at first. The lady above me was nice and she loved to play her old school music, which didn't bother me a bit. The man across from her was so funny he was always cracking jokes and keeping it "live." There were two men who occupied the two apartments in the back and they were very laid back. Everyone made me feel at home. They often brought food home from neighboring restaurants for me to try, assuring me that southern food was the best, and we would often sit outside on the steps and laugh and talk for hours. This really helped because at first I was having a hard time not being around my mom and siblings.

Majority of the residents there were a part of the US Army and its military base was less than a mile away. I am a pretty private person and I stay to myself in terms of being at home. I was never really the "neighborly" type. In Kansas I was very friendly and would always speak, but I can't tell you more than two of my former neighbors name from my adulthood. I knew their faces and we would grin and wave and sometimes comment on the weather, but that was about it. So that fact that I was sitting outside and talking to them was out of the norm for me. I still would drift away and would go back into my one bedroom apartment and just relax. I like it quiet unless I am playing music or entertaining guests. Other than that I am content. It wasn't out of the ordinary for one of the neighbors to knock on my door and ask me to come out and quit being "anti-social" as they would always say jokingly. And sometimes I would come on out. This really was a bunch of great people all of them older in their late forties or older, so I loved that because there was never any nonsense going on in our building.

As I was saying in pat one (Hephzibah), everything was great at first but after awhile I found myself asking God if this move was really something I should've done. Sure I was in an area where a lot of social things were going on, and I could travel a few hours in each direction and be in a major city, or a "to do" area. That wasn't the problem and the people were not the problem. I was allowing negative people from my past to set me up for failure. I allowed their "O you'll be back" comments to resonate so loud that it drowned out the voice of God. When I began to get back into my word and seek God and he told me to do the research on where I was, the revelation brought such healing and excitement to me. I almost allowed someone else's will for my life overpower what God had for me.

The Definition

pin·na·cle
pin·na·cle [pínnək'l]
n (plural pin·na·cles)

1. **highest point: the highest or topmost point or level
   of something** *at the pinnacle of a career*
2. **geography mountain peak: a natural peak, especially
   a distinctively pointed one on a mountain or in a
   mountain range**

*Encarta ® World English Dictionary © & (P) 1998-2004
Microsoft Corporation. All rights reserved.*

The Revelation

Psalm 95

New International Version (NIV)
*1 Come, let us sing for joy to the Lord; let us shout aloud
to the Rock of our salvation. 2 Let us come before him with
thanksgiving
and extol him with music and song. 3 For the Lord is the
great God,
the great King above all gods. 4 In his hand are the depths of
the earth, and the mountain peaks belong to him.*

God had taken me to my highest point and though I was
dwelling there day in and day out I didn't even notice. I
had finally reached my mountain top, exactly where God
promised me I would be, and I couldn't even see it. God is
saying trust me, I cannot lie. If I said I am going to do it
then you will see it come true. Understanding that this was

not my final destination, I believe I was placed there as a reminder that this move was ordained by God. Here I was residing at Pinnacle Place in Hephzibah. The high place, the mountain peak in which I can find God's delight, and I did not even realize it! Psalm ninety-five reminded me that even the mountain peaks (Pinnacle) belonged to Him and I was still in His hand and right where he wanted to be. As I stated in part one, some may call this another coincidence but I believe this was God's way of speaking to me and confirming that this was exactly where I was supposed to be and that he was still in control. AMEN!

Shout it out

When life comes at you with its crazy schemes
Know that you maintain the victory indeed
Turn your pressure into praise
Your sorrows into serenity
Shout it out

When people are talking about you more than they are
praying for you
When your friends and family become few
Stand with dignity
And declare to the adversary this too shall pass
Shout it out

When your money is short and your bills are long
When everything in your life seems to be going wrong
Shout it out
Shout it out
Shout it out

When your flesh is weak, know that all your needs He
can meet
Despite of what you are going through, know that the
God you serve is true
Shout it out
Shout it out
Shout it out

Turn your pressure into praise
Your sorrows into serenity
Stand with dignity
And declare to the adversary this too shall pass

Sing
Hallelujah
Out loud
Until
Triumph comes

Shout it out
Shout it out
Shout it out

Woman of Promise & Strength

To every woman who has an "I can make it" attitude

To every woman who has destiny in her belly, and a plan on her mind

To every woman who strives to succeed despite the cost

To every woman who has haters on her back, and victory in her heart

To every woman who has struggled to the top

To every woman who is spending her last day at the bottom

To every woman that has a dream that she will not let die

You, my sista are a woman of promise & strength

Stand tall-Look forward-Press forth

Refreshed

I awaken in the morning with a smile on my face
What a blessin' it is to see another day
A song of joy fills my heart, my steps are quickened by its beat.
For I am living victoriously, no longer in defeat.
Such a change has come over me, it seems everything is at its best.
No more sadness, no more tears. I have been refreshed

The feeling is captivating, and I don't want it to pass
I am in agreement with Dr. King, "I am free at last."
It's like an ice cold drink on a hot summer's day
Or like the dew in the morning, that the sun will dry away.
So much gladness, so much joy. No longer am I depressed
It's as if a weight has been lifted. I have been refreshed

There has been a rejuvenation of my spirit, a renewing of my mind
A restoring of my faith and reviving of my finances, all right on time
It is finally my time! It's finally my season!
I am so glad I didn't give in, so happy that I passed the test
Or I would have never known how it feels to be refreshed

It's like standing under a rushing waterfall, I feel my blessings pouring down
The same feeling you get when you win a gold medal, a ribbon, or a crown
It's a moment in life that no one can take away
The reward you receive when you keep the faith, fast and pray
God did exactly what He said, I found his word to be true
I am living proof that there is no limit to what God can do

The feeling is so amazing it brings tears of joy to my eyes
As I reminisce on how it use to be, always cloudy dark skies
I am so grateful, I have so much to be thankful for
I received everything that was taken from me and so much more
You can't understand my praise, I tried to explain it, I did my best
I hope you can somewhat comprehend the way I felt the day that I was refreshed

Victory Lane

On your mark! Get set, go!
The gun sounds and the race begins
Full speed ahead I go 'cause I don't want to be at the end
Over this hurdle around this corner, this competition is
intense
None of my opponents are backing down their sweat is
the evidence

The crowd is cheering their respective runner along
Encouraging them that they can do it and that they are
not alone
Go, go, go, they yell from the stands
Using loud objects to get their attention and waving
things around in their hands

Faster, faster look straight ahead they exclaim
Getting furious at their participant calling them out by
name
You can do it I heard another one say
But as I looked in front of me, the finish line seemed so
far away

Some of the candidates have dropped out of the race
Though they had people supporting them, they did not
believe they had what it takes
I could see the end but I had no clue what it was going to be
When I make it to the finish line, will there be a medal
for me?

I can never give up is what I kept telling myself
Self-satisfaction is worth more than recognition and
wealth
So I pushed harder ran faster and to my surprise
I began passing the others whom I was far behind

Almost there—I passed a sign reading "This way to
victory lane!"
As I got closer, I saw another sign that read my name
There I could see my loved ones cheering me on at the
finish line
So I picked up speed and before I knew it, I had finished
the race
However, no other participants were around me I had
taken first place

I waited to see who would be second runner up and who
would be number three
But no one ever showed and the prizes were awarded to
me
You see sometimes life has us running on the same track
just for a distance
Everyone is not always going in your direction, just run
your race with persistence

Do not worry about those around you as their course
may change
Stay focused on your goal and look and listen for your
name.
If you don't make it to the finish line you are the only one
to blame
You will make it if you try, just remember its "This way
to victory lane!"

The Painting

I'd like to paint a picture although I cannot draw
I would not base it on other pictures, just on what I saw
I'd paint a yellow sun in the sky and make it give off a
bright light
I put some clouds and some birds up there too, to set the
sky off just right

If I could paint a picture it would be wide and free
I'd show all the flowers the valleys the rivers and the
streams
If I could paint a picture I'd make it as beautiful as can be
I'd add detail after detail and make it a reflection of me

I want to paint a picture but I'm not Leonardo or Picasso
All the tricks and the correct procedures of this craft I do
not know
This masterpiece I want to paint is intriguing and unique
Like Mona Lisa, I will be remembered by this piece

Life is a canvas and your dreams are the paint
The paintbrush is your actions, if you do nothing it will
remain blank
I've been painting a picture all my life
I hope that when others see it they say I did it right

When others see my painting what will they see?
Was I kind to others, did I pursue my dreams?
Is there a lot of love in the painting? For anything did I
take a stand?
Does my painting have any color to it or is it just bland?

When they see my painting does it seem vain?
Will they see me giving to others I did not know by
name?
Does it depict the labor of my hands and the sores on
my feet?
The pains of my persistence because I would not accept
defeat

I've been painting a picture all my life
I hope that when others see it they say I did it right
The reality of it is that you're painting a picture too.
Make sure you paint it like you want it to appear, there is
no redo

I'm painting a picture although I cannot draw
Like a mural it will stand wide and tall
Loving, dreaming, doing, and having lots of fun
Taking good care of my canvas, because I only get one

Terms of Endearment

Everyone loves to be called nice names. It reminds us of our good qualities, boosts our esteem, makes us feel good, or perhaps just makes our day. When people say things like good morning beautiful, or how are you today handsome? It seems to just give us a feeling that we are noticed and maybe sometime even feelings of appreciation. Maybe you have been called sweetie, dear, honey, darling, suga, or perhaps baby. Whatever name you have been called, when you hear it, it really does something to you, especially if it comes from the mouth of the ones we love or have an interest in. When we hear these words our smiles get so large, that every tooth in our mouth is showing or we get to the point where the color of our skin has lightened by an entire shade. Then you have your family members, close friends and significant others that give you those special names that only they are allowed to call you. Names like buga, pookie, pinky, Meme, Nana, shorty, Paulie, or fat-fat. A familiar sound that when it is heard you know that they have to know you. And depending on what they call you, you know where they know you from even if you can't see their face. You are sure of it because those nicknames mean something. And only those close to you can call you "meatloaf" and get away with it because they know the story behind it and really they are saying it out of love. It is a symbol of their affection to you that confirms the closeness of relationship that you really have with them. They are known as terms of endearment, or expressions of affection.

God is the same way. He loves for His name to be called. He loves for us to remind Him of who He is. Calling him by His name is a form of worship and praise. Simply calling God Holy, Awesome, or Mighty, takes Him to that same level of comfort you feel when someone calls you beautiful or handsome. And just like most of us He has several names. He is known by different names to different people. It lets Him know where we know Him from. He can tell by what we call Him just how close of a relationship we have with Him, or by the tone of our voice, if it's a name we know Him by or that we heard someone else call Him and just picked up on.

Some say that He is Jehovah Jireh, God the Provider. Some say he is Jehovah Nissi, God of Victory. Some call him Ropha, The Healer. Some call Him Abba, Father, another a Comforter, another The Prince of Peace, and many other names. When He hears these names He knows why we are calling Him that and He is reminded that we haven't forgotten just how good He really is. Whatever God has been to you or done for you, make sure that you are calling Him by that name. Understanding, that it is worship, just as you want to hear how much you are loved and appreciated so does God. You don't have to get fancy and creative just tell Him who He is. Remind Him of His goodness and faithfulness. Since He inhabits in the praise of His people, invite Him in by opening up your mouth in worship and sup with the Lord on a daily basis and not only when you are in a worship service. Don't be a carbon copy of someone else, make it personal. Just like you'll always be pookie to your grandma no matter what, God says He will always be whatever you need Him to be, just say the name.

God is interested in who you know him to be. If you remember in Mark 8:27-29 and Luke 9:18-20, when Jesus asked his disciples who the crowds and other people around were calling Him. And they told Him, some call you Elijah, and some John the Baptist or another prophet, and Jesus asked them, "But who do you say that I am?" I am sure the disciples had looks of astonishment on their face. The Bible doesn't tell us if everyone said something later, it only tells us what Peter's reply was. Peter replied "you are the Messiah!" When you are in worship God is not concerned about what others call Him or what you may have heard, He wants to know who He is to you. And like Peter a true worshiper has to be ready to enter into conversation with God alone, even when a crowd is around! He responded immediately to Jesus' question. Take a few moments and think about all of the things that God has been, and is to you. Are you prepared to answer the question that Jesus asked His disciples? Don't call God by a name you heard by association God is asking, ***"But who do you say that I am?"***

Mark 8:27-29
New International Version (NIV)

[27] *Jesus and his disciples went on to the villages around Caesarea Philippi. On the way he asked them, "Who do people say I am?"* [28] *They replied, "Some say John the Baptist; others say Elijah; and still others, one of the prophets."* [29] *"But what about you?" he asked. "Who do you say I am?" Peter answered, "You are the Messiah."*

You Kept Me

When the pressures of life weighed so heavily on my
shoulders that I almost lost my mind
When everything around me seemed to produce chaos and
there seemed to be no peace
> You Kept Me

When close friends and family members I loved dearly
betrayed me without cause
When people took unmerited and untrue stabs at my
character in an attempt to destroy me
> You Kept Me

When the economy crashed and the recession arose and
bills flooded in and money did not
When my dreams seemed like a fairy tale that would never
come true and I wanted to give up
> You Kept Me

When discouragement reigned and I was told I wasn't
good enough
When my heart seemed to be broken just as often as it beat
> You Kept Me

When the enemy was but a few steps away and others
around me were affected
When danger was present and death looked me square in
the eyes and I should've lost my life
> You Kept Me

O Lord what a "Keeper" You are! You Kept Me!

Every Now and Then

The melodic song the birds sing early in the morning
The sweet fragrance of the most beautiful flower
The bustling of the multi-colored leaves
The swaying of the bright green grass in the many fields

A soft breeze of the fresh wind
The heat of the sun beating down on my face
The reflections of life I see in the many bodies of water
The sound of children at play

The taste of falling raindrops
The stillness of the night
The twinkling of the brightest star
The fullness of the moon

Every now and then I think of you
Morning noon and night
Every now and then you are on my mind
There always seems to be something that reminds me of
you
Every now and then

Truth Be Told

Truth be told—you are not as strong as you say you are
Your knees sometimes buckle and your heart skips a beat
Your eyes sometime water at the thought of defeat

Truth be told—you are not as wise as you think
You've made decisions that you wish would remain secret
You've said things you are not proud of because you spoke
to quick

Truth be told—you are not as confident as you portray
You demoralize others on a quest to find your identity
and to boost yourself esteem
You embellish your stories and accomplishments in an
attempt to disguise your own insecurities

Truth be told—none of us are perfect we all require daily
grooming
Our biggest flaw is mistreating one another and not
discovering the facts but instead assuming

Truth be told—overcoming our weaknesses makes us
stronger
Learning from our past experiences gives us wisdom
Recognizing our insecurities helps us to conquer them
and love ourselves more so that we can properly love one
another

Truth be told—you are more important than you think
and we need each other to survive
This world can be a cold cruel place that we can change
one day at a time
But only if the truth be told!

Spring Water

Cool refreshing purified
Crisp untainted fortified
If used improperly will make you horrified
Therefore majority of its request must be nullified

Precious rare irreplaceable
Its beauty indescribable
Its true worth is undeniable
Its look its smell its taste very desirable

You see "spring water" is the freshest water, the best in its
class
Yet because he told you that you were beautiful and that
he loved you. You offered him a glass

Naive to the fact that once he dips into your well it will
never be pure again, that you won't get a chance to do it
over, once you pour it out, that's the end

Unaware that once he has tasted of your springs and his
thirst has been quenched, there is no reason for him to
return to you of your substance he has been drenched

So on to new adventures he will go to spy out new land
But devastated empty confused and grimy you stand

Hold tight to your spring water and never be ashamed
That you are still in possession of the gift you acquired
when you received your name

Guard your spring water don't be afraid to reject those
that are just passing by
Wait on the one who wants to forever remain and
understands you are more than meets the eye

Cool refreshing purified
Crisp untainted fortified
If used improperly will make you horrified
Therefore majority of its request must be nullified

Precious rare irreplaceable
Its beauty indescribable
Its true worth is undeniable
Make your spring water unavailable

A Bed of Roses

Though nobody knows your name, you are always on the
program and often working behind the scenes
Though nobody gives you praise, you are always there
and do what you do from your heart not for recognition
Though nobody remembers your struggle, you continue
to press forward forgetting about the things that were
once on your personal to do list
Though nobody honors your sacrifices, you unselfishly
continue to give all that you have and half of what you do
not have to ensure the happiness of those around you
Though great will be your reward in heaven it would be
nice to get a few things today
Though this is not enough, I want to tell you thank you
and let you know how much you are appreciated
Though I don't always make the time, I wanted to set
aside a moment for you to let you know that without
your presence in my life I am nothing
Though it's not much, I gathered some words from the
barrels of my heart and soul and tried to combine them
to make since. To tell you how much I love you and how
in my life you've been such a gift
Though I can never repay you I want to die trying, I want
to make you proud so that you will know that all you
gave up was not in vain. That your many sleepless nights
and restless days were for my personal gain
Though you never complain, always seem to know what
to say, there is something you have yet to discover.

There is no greater accomplishment, nothing I am more
proud of in all of my living than I am grateful to God for
having you as my mother
If I picked a flower for every tear you have wiped away,
the advice, the gifts and the guidance too
It would cover every hill, every valley, every forest every
street, yes the only thing the world would see is you
So I decided to give you your flowers while you are yet
living so that you may smell them while it is day
Instead of one day writing flowery words with grief and
carrying rose filled wreaths to cover your then dead body
in your grave
Since it is impossible for me to pick you a flower for
everything you do and have done from the very start
I decided to plant the seeds from the flowers you've sown
and grow them in my heart
It has often been said that "life is not a bed of roses" and
I use to believe that was true, but as I began to reflect on
all of your beauty and grace and your smiling face and I
realized whoever made that statement, never met you

Reflection

Reflect

1. To send something back: to redirect something that strikes a surface, especially light, sound, or heat, usually back toward its point of origin
Encarta ® World English Dictionary © & (P) 1998-2004 Microsoft Corporation. All rights reserved.

Reflection

1. A careful thought, especially the process of reconsidering previous actions, events, or decisions
Encarta ® World English Dictionary © & (P) 1998-2004 Microsoft Corporation. All rights reserved.

Genesis 1:26-27
New International Version (NIV)

26 *Then God said, "Let us make mankind in our image, in our likeness, so that they may rule over the fish in the sea and the birds in the sky, over the livestock and all the wild animals, [a] and over all the creatures that move along the ground."*

27 *So God created mankind in his own image, in the image of God he created them; male and female he created them.*

~*Prayer of Reflection*~

Dear Heavenly Father, Creator of the universe,
Thank you for being Lord of all in my life
God, it is so easy to get caught up in things and people
that are around, when I do not make the proper time for
you.
From the beginning of time you have told me who I was
and that I was created in your image.
That means that from my mouth I should only speak
your words
That my hands should do your work
And that I should go out and spread the good news
Yet somewhere along the way I was sidetracked and for
that Lord I am sorry.
Forgive me for not being a replica of you at all times
Because I am the reflection of you that the world can see
So Father I redirect my mind, my body, my spirit and my
praise back to you
And from this day forth I will be a constant reminder to
the dying world that you still live.
In Jesus Name
Amen

~PSALMS (SONGS)~

Divine Purpose

(The Song)
Genesis 1:27 and Romans 14:11

Lead

I was created in your image. I was designed to give you praise.

You sent your son to buy my pardon, so that I may one day see your face.

From dust you formed me breathed the breath of life into me. So that I may worship your name.

Chorus

This is my divine (my divine) purpose

(My divine) My divine (divine) purpose

This is my divine (my divine) purpose

My purpose is to worship your name.

Lead

Forgive me Father, for I have sinned, Strayed so far away from my original assignment. Stepped out of your will attempting to create my own. Forgetting my purpose is to bring glory to your thrown.

Chorus

This is my divine (my divine) purpose

(My divine) My divine (divine) purpose

This is my divine (my divine) purpose

My purpose is to worship your name.

Vamp

You are so worthy of my praise I will lift up holy hands and bless your name
Praise and honor I give unto you, because my purpose is to worship your name. (2xs)

Chorus

This is my divine (my divine) purpose
(My divine) My divine (divine) purpose
This is my divine (my divine) purpose
My purpose is to worship your name.

D.A.N.C.E

Lead

Brotha's and sista's let me tell ya, it's alright to praise his name

There's nothing to it, all you gotta do is do it. No two people have to praise Him the same. For the Bible says that even David danced, he danced so hard he came out his clothes. And what a shame it would be, not to get out our seats, because we we're too ashamed to let it show.

Chorus

Dance-dance it's alright to praise Him. Get out of yo seat move to this holy beat. Come on and dance while you have a chance. Hallelujah!

Lead

Let everything that has breath praise the Lord. Praise Him for all He's done. He's given life, love, health, strength, a job, every meal, even paid the bills, you oughta give Him some praise. But if your too ashamed then the rocks will cry out. I don't won't none cryin' for me. And if I can't praise Him down here O my Lord, how do I expect to live in eternity. (Come on and dance)

Chorus

Dance-dance it's alright to praise Him. Get out of yo seat move to this holy beat. Come on and dance while you have a chance. Hallelujah!

Bridge

When the praises go up blessings come down. Lord shower down your blessings on me. 'Cause when I think of all you've done, I get the David mentality.

Vamp

*So we can *lean wit it rock wit it* on one accord, because *O I think they like me* but I know He loves me more. He's no *ordinary people* he's so *unpredictable.* If we can *1-2 step* with Ciara guess what? We can take 3 steps for Jesus sho nuf'. So get on your feet and give my God the Glory!

Chorus

Dance-dance it's alright to praise Him. Get out of yo seat move to this holy beat. Come on and dance while you have a chance. Hallelujah!

Special

So bow down your head and lift your hands to the sky. Now bend yo body and move your legs from side to side. Come on and dance, dance, dance, dance, dance while you have the chance Hallelujah!

D is for Desire Him
A is for Adore Him
N is don't you dare have No other God's before Him
C is for Confess Him
E is for Exalt Him

Dance, dance, dance, dance, while you have chance.

Chorus

Dance-dance it's alright to praise Him. Get out of yo seat move to this holy beat. Come on and dance while you have a chance. Hallelujah!

You Can Make It

Chorus

You can make it—yes you can make it (4xs)

Verse one

You can make it through the storm
You can make it through the rain
You can make through the heartache
You can make it through the pain
You can make it—Yes you can

Chorus

You can make it—yes you can make it (4xs)

Verse two

You can make it through the lies
You can make it through the deceit
You can make through dark skies
You can make it through the defeat
You can make it—Yes you can

Chorus

You can make it—yes you can make it (4xs)
You can make it
You can make it
You can make it
Yes you can

Rosetta

Dedicated to my grandmother on her 69th Birthday

Verse one

I see your life and I can't help but cry
Strength love and wisdom it shows in your eyes
I know no one who loves quite like u do
So proud to call you grandma, I love you yes I do

Chorus

Rosetta you're all the world to me
Ro—o-o-osettaa I love u more than I sing
Ro-o-o-setta taught me the meaning of family
Taught me how to dream the reason I believe . . . Rosetta

Verse two

When I see u, I see a woman who survived
So many things the lost of her siblings, and a child
How do I repay all of the love you give to me?
More than an inheritance but a legacy you will leave

Chorus

Rosetta you're all the world to me
Ro—o-o-osettaa I love u more than I sing
Ro-o-o-setta taught me the meaning of family
Taught me how to dream the reason I believe . . . Rosetta

So proud to call you Grandma, Rosetta I love U yes I
do . . . yes I do

Lord I Give My Praise to You

I can't breathe without cha
Can't move—can't live without cha
Lord I give my praise to you
(Ut o Ut o)

Lead
Every time I think of your goodness I can't help but sing
I can't explain it, I can't contain it, Lord you been so good
to me (Oh ooO)

Declaration
I can't breathe without cha
I can't move without cha
I can't live without cha
Lord I give my praise to you

Oh o oh oh o
Lead
Every step I take every move I make it's all because of you
You're so worthy, of my praise, so lifted hands I'll raise (O
Lord)

Declaration
I can't breathe without cha
I can't move without cha
I can't live without cha
Lord I give my praise to you
Oh o oh oh o

Bridge
No o oh o no o oh o, I can't do it without cha
No o oh o, no oh ooO oh Lord I give my praise to you
(repeat)

Oh o oh oh o

Declaration
I can't breathe without cha
I can't move without cha
I can't live without cha
Lord I give my praise to you

Oh o oh oh o

No (5xs) No (6xs) I can't make it without cha (can't make
it without cha)
No (6xs) No oh ooooh o oh Lord I give my praise to you
(repeat)

Oh o oh oh o

I can't breathe without cha
Can't move—can't live without cha
Lord I give my praise to you
(Ut o Ut o)

I can't breathe without cha
Can't move—can't live without cha
Lord I give my praise to you
(Ut o Ut o)

What Are You Selling?

If you look around you no matter where you are something is for sale. Even if you are driving down a highway there are billboards that remind you that gas and food are coming up in the next exit or two, or that you can pull over to come visit some great attraction. Marketing and advertisement are there to get the consumers attention and to quickly point out the features and benefits of their product or service in such a way that the consumer feels that they need to have it. Jingles and slogans fill the radio stations and television commercials with catchy verbiage and quick beats to remind you just how easy and hassle free having their product or service will make your life or how it will enhance your current situation. The lyrics are rarely profound and the beat is always up tempo and is designed to keep you humming long after the commercial is over, so that you can share with others what you have just heard.

I have been asked frequently by numerous women the infamous question, "why can't I find a good man blah blah blah? I responded with "let the man find you," as my mother and other godly women have always told me. Referring to Proverbs 18:22, "He who finds a wife finds a good thing, and obtains favor from the Lord.(NIV)" I had always been taught that it's the man's job to do the finding, and in my waiting to be found I should be preparing myself to be a great wife, mother, and help-mate. I was taught that I should carry myself as a lady if I want to attract gentlemen and that when I dress I should leave something to the imagination and not put it all on display for everyone to see, as prostitutes do. I was constantly told that a real man is looking for a woman with more than full time lover on her resume', and that if that's the first thing a man asks for I should "run like hell!" I thought what world are they living in? Most times if you are not dressing sexy or at least acting as if there is a chance for sex to happen you get overlooked. That's another story entirely. Needless to say, you live and you learn and you wish you would have simply just taken the advice you were given in the beginning and saved yourself a lot of headaches and heartache! It's most certainly true that if you stand in the rain long enough you will definitely get wet! The same is true when it comes to how you carry yourself.

I honestly wanted to give them the answers they were looking for, as it is a wonderful thing to be happily married and reunited with the man God designed for especially for you. But as I observed I saw women wearing clothes that showed more than it covered. I heard language even a sailor would be ashamed to say coming from their mouths. I witnessed women bragging about hobbies and talents that only their husband should know about, and saying it in public places as if is cute or acceptable behavior. I see the names women call themselves on Facebook, Twitter, license plates and even tattoos. Names like; "Ms Thick thighs, juicy booty, the baddest B*%&#," and it gets worse. Ladies my heart goes out to you today. Who was it that taught you that is who you were and how you were to be identified? With an attitude like this, your name is sure to remain on the "baby mama" list and never on the "Mrs. Or the Wifey" list! You will always be the woman on the side until you decide that you are worth more! Come on ladies you are more than that and when you start to respect yourself then, he will respect you!

I'm not just sharing this from a woman's point of view. I happen to know some real men who are just tiered of women thinking that's all they want! Men who are actually being chased and pursued for sex because somehow our minds have been programmed that, that this is the way to get and keep a man. Don't get me wrong I know that there are a lot of guys who are really like that. But we should separate those guys when considering the man we want to spend the rest of my life with, there is a huge difference. Of course men enjoy sex, but when it comes down to finding a wife, someone they want to spend their life with, they are looking for something Victoria's Secret does not sell! Ladies do not be deceived, just because he wears a business suit doesn't make him husband material. You have to start looking beyond the financial and the outside facade of the package, and get right to the heart of things. As my Pastor Sammy James says, "don't fall for Bozo while waiting on Boaz!"

I just want to correct whomever it was that told you to dress and behave in these manners. They are wrong. You are queens and a queen must be in character at all times. If you want to be treated as royalty you must act like royalty. News flash, men are going to buy what you advertise! You can't present yourself as easy which is what u are doing when you degrade yourself, and expect prince charming to want to walk shoulder to shoulder with you! You are in charge of your commercial. You can't advertise a dirty mop and get mad when scum responds to the add!

Remember, your jingle (how you present yourself, the first impression) will continue to resound in their heads long after you walk away. You have the power to present your features and benefits and they should not be sexual at all. You are probably familiar with the old school saying that a real man wants a "lady in the streets and a freak in the sheets!" In other words carry yourself like a lady in public at all times. And what you and your husband do at home is your business and your business only! Respect yourself ladies, you are so worth it!

I am Healed

By His stripes I'm healed
(Whoa oh O oh whoa)
Victory I can feel
(I feel such a freedom)
I have been made whole
(I've been restored)
Got my healing
It's all over me
I am healed
(2xs)

I'm healed
(By his blood I've been redeemed)
I'm healed
(No longer captive I am free indeed)
I'm healed
(I gave it over to God and He)
Touch me
(2xs)

(Yeah Yay Yeah yay)

By His stripes I'm healed
(Whoa oh O oh whoa)
Victory I can feel
(I feel such a freedom)
I have been made whole
(I've been restored)
Got my healing
It's all over me
I am healed

Rainy Days

Verse one

How would I know you as a healer, if I never had been sick?

How would I know you as Jireh, if I'd never been broke?

How would I know that you were a comforter, if you never had to wipe away my tears?

I didn't understand it then, but now it all makes sense. The rain had to come for the sun to shine again.

Verse two

How could I praise you with my whole heart, if I never seen a cloudy day (and)

How could I love you as a savior, if you never had to save me from anything?

How could I give myself to you freely, if you never proved just who you are?

I didn't understand it then, but now it all makes sense. The rain had to come for the sun to shine again.

Vamp

RAIN I get my joy through THE RAIN my peace comes in THE RAIN deliverance is in THE RAIN OOH.

Lord thank you for the pain and thank you for the rain—Lord thank you for my rainy days

False Ending by Lead
Lord thank you for my rainy
Thank you for my rainy
Thank you for my rainy days

Vamp
RAIN I get my joy through THE RAIN my peace comes in THE RAIN deliverance is in THE RAIN OOH. (Keep adlibbing and modulating) (Repeat)
Lord thank you for the pain and thank you for the rain—Lord thank you for my rainy days

Lead
Oh o oh Ooooh I didn't understand it then, but now it all makes sense. The rain had to come for the sun to shine again.

He Said He Would Supply

Chorus
He said He would supply
God said he would supply
All of my needs—according to His riches in Glory
If I obey~ If I have Faith~ The size of a mustard seed
(ummm um um um uuummm then) He'll supply my
need

Verse One
If He clothes the grass in the fields
Makes sure the birds and the bees never miss a meal
How much more will He do for me.
Created in His image—designed for eternity
If he said (then) I believe it—Jesus will Supply
Not only my needs but also my heart's desire

Chorus
He said He would supply
God said he would supply
All of my needs—according to His riches in Glory
If I obey~ If I have Faith~ The size of a mustard seed
(ummm um um um uuummm then) He'll supply my need
He'll supply my need—He'll supply my need

Lead Breakdown
I know it cause he did it for me
Now I'm walking victoriously—(he'll supply the need)
Released Daniel from the lion's den
For Job, He restored everything
Stepped in the furnace for the Hebrew boys
(He'll supply the need)

He gave sight to the blind
And strength to the weak
And from a little sack lunch he created a feast
Just ask and receive
Have faith and believe

Ending
Just ask and receive
Have faith and believe
Then He'll supply the need

Everything

Chorus
You're my everything, all praise I'll give to you <When
I get dark cloud I see the sun shine through> o You're
my everything and there is none like you. You're my
everything. (ooooh)You're my everything.

**When I think of your goodness, and all you've done
for me
I can't help but to praise ya—because you're so worthy.
Despite of my trials, no matter how much I've been,
untrue
You were always there, you were the one who brought
me through (that's why)**

Chorus
You're my everything and there is none like you, <When
I get dark cloud I see the sun shine through> o You're
my everything and there is none like you. You're my
everything. (ooooh)You're my everything.

**I am so thankful—for Lord you've been so kind
Throughout my many dark days—you've been my,
sunshine
You are Jehovah Shalom—you gave me peace of mind
Sho' nuff Jehovah Nissi you are victorious every time
(for you)**

Chorus

You're my everything and there is none like you, <When I get dark cloud I see the sun shine through> o You're my everything and there is none like you. You're my everything. (ooooh)You're my everything.

You Did It All for Me

Chorus/or Lead

You did it all
You did it all
You did it all for me way back on Calvary
You did it all
You did it all
Lord I thank you 'cause you did it all for me.

REPEAT

Tag

You did it
You did it
You did it
All
(repeat & modulate)
You did it all for me

Lead

Lord I thank you 'cause you did it all
Thank you 'cause you did it all
I thank you cause you did it all for me
All for me
All for me—yeah yeah yes
Lord thank you 'cause you did it all for me

Destiny Chaser

Life is full of surprises. I have done and said a lot of things in my life that I am not proud of. Some things that I wish I could have a chance to do over, others I just rejoice that I made it through, because my choices were so foolish they could have, and should have led to more severe consequences. In life there is no such thing as a rewind button. Once you speak it into the atmosphere, you can never take it back. I am so glad that when I look back at my "yesterday," it looks nothing like my today and it is so far from my tomorrow!

As I matured I leaned and understood that everything in my past actually prepared me for my future. It toughened my skin, produced patience, and strengthened my self esteem. However, people have a way of showcasing the shame in your life. They use phrases like "remember when or don't act like you forgot." Sometime it's because of jealousy, other times is because they use to have such a great relationship with you and now that you have moved on, they don't see themselves in your future, so they try to remind you of how it use to be—the good ole days!

Despite of what you may have said or done in your past. Regardless of all the things people can remind you of, that may be unpleasant. Don't allow yesterday's guilt, to sabotage your future. You have to be willing to pursue your dreams at all cost. Be a destiny chaser. Make a commitment to yourself that you will not stop until you get to the place in life you've always dreamed. Do not look back until you cross the finish line! And once you reach your goal only turn around long enough to remind yourself of how far you have made it, and how many obstacles you have overcome.

Life is about choices. You have the right to choose the direction and the speed in which you run this race. Do not let who you "use to be" keep you from becoming who you were "destined to be." When chasing your destiny don't be afraid to run pass those family members and friends who want to keep you in your "yesterday!" Remember the tests of yesterday so that you will not have to repeat them today. Use the wisdom of today to help prepare you for tomorrow. Embrace your change and chase after the things you have dreamed about for so long. Today is your day run hard and fast, your destiny awaits you!

The Way of the World

Killing, stealing, abusing, neglecting
Crime scenes, homelessness, discrimination is at its best
Recession, war, still no money for the poor
What happen to humanity?

World hunger, inequality, poor health care,
disappointment
Political schemes, disrespect, the unemployment rate is
ridiculous
Pirates, terrorist, seems no one's making a difference
What happen to the dream?

Is it too late to come together?
Or will we always fight each other
I know that if we really tried
We could change the direction of things
But (spoken)
I guess it's just way of the world
Ooooh ooO hoo
I guess it's just way of the world
Ooooh ooO hoo

O when will people see
That we are all created equally
Please tell me what is it gonna take
To show everybody it doesn't matter what your race

Your social status shouldn't matter to me
Neither whether you're wearing Faded Glory or Gucci
It's about time for us to open our eyes
Time to embrace one another, all man kind
But (spoken)
I guess it's just way of the world
Ooooh ooO hoo
I guess it's just way of the world
Ooooh ooO hoo
I guess it's just way of the world
I guess it's just way of the world
I guess it's just way of the world
I guess it's just way of the world

God help us! (Spoken)

Dream on

You can be whatever you want to be
A doctor, a lawyer, even a movie star
There's no limit to what you can do
You can get there if you believe

Hook
Don't stop dreamin'
Dream on
Despite of what others think
You can be who you wanna be
Don't stop dreamin'
Dream on
If you really wanna succeed . . . you gotta dream

There is so much power in dreaming
In it there are no limits
You set the parameters, you are in full control
An astronaut, a teacher yes, an entertainer
When you dream, there's nothing that's out of your reach

Don't stop dreamin'
Dream on
Despite of what others think
You can be who you wanna be
Don't stop dreamin'
Dream on
If you really wanna succeed . . . you gotta dream

Sho Nuf

Verse one

Today is the day, I can finally say
That I found someone, who completes me in everyway
He adores me, treats me like his queen
He never puts his hands on me, the type of guy out of a
movie scene

Now this man I speak of is Mr. Right
And the best thing about this man is that he's mine

Chorus

This man that I speak of, he wipes away all my tears
He holds me so tight, removes everyone of my fears
A gentleman at heart, with a pinch of thug on the side
I sho nuf I love my man. I sho nuf love my man.

Verse two

Gifts for reason, long walks in the park
Flowers and candy coming straight from his heart
And yes he's a dreamer, but never loses sight with reality
O how I love him and my baby loves me

Now this man I speak of is Mr. Right
And the best thing about this man is that he's mine

Chorus
This man that I speak of, he wipes away all my tears
He holds me so tight, removes everyone of my fears
A gentleman at heart with a pinch of thug on the side
I sho nuf I love my man. I sho nuf love my man.

Lead
Now this man I speak of is Mr. Right
And the best thing about this man is that he's mine

Vamp
I love this man
I need this man
Gotta this man
Sho nuf

Psalm 47

Oh clap your hands all ye people—shout with a voice of triumph
For the Lord Most High—He is awesome

Sing praises to our God
Sing praises to our King
He is the King of all the earth
Sing praises to our God

He is greatly exalted
He is worthy to be praised
He is greatly exalted
Sing praises to our God
Sing praises to our King

He reigns over every nation—and he sits on His holy throne
There is none like Him—Give praise to Him alone

Sing praises to our God
Sing praises to our King
He is the King of all the earth
Sing praises to our God

He is greatly exalted
He is worthy to be praised
He is greatly exalted
Sing praises to our God
Sing praises to our King

Clap your hands cause he's worthy of the honor
Clap your hands cause he's worthy of the praise
Lift up at shout with a voice of triumph
He is King of all the earth—exalt his name
(Repeat)

Release

The storm is raging, and
The wind is blowing
The waves are rising, and
Making it hard for me to see

Lord I know you can send peace to calm this storm
Lord please send release

Re-lease, Re-lease
Holy Spirit Release
I can't make it without your help
O Lord, release

Savor the Flavor of God's Favor

Have you ever walked into someone's house or a restaurant and took a big whiff of what was cooking and asked the question, "what is that smell?" and once they answer you, you usually follow with the response, "um that smells good!" Although you didn't know exactly what they had on the stove the aroma filled the room and quickly your nostrils and your brain told you it was something good. Nine times out of ten, when your taste buds get a taste of what your nose has already been enjoying, it's just as good or even better than you imagined. That is how it is when you come in contact with someone who is favored by God. You do not always know what it is automatically, but you can sense something about them, there is a different aroma that filled the room once they entered it and it smells good. It is the smell of Favor and God is the Master chef!

In one form or another we have all come in contact with favor. The dictionary defines favor as an act of kindness performed or granted out of goodwill or preferential treatment shown to somebody. Most of us have our own favorites, our favorite, color, food or song. Or perhaps you have been the teacher's favorite or a favorite to a family member, either way there is nothing like receiving your favorite things or being in the presence of the one who favors you because of that special treatment you receive. Nothing can be compared to the favor of God.

Not even grace or mercy. It is almost an indescribable feeling.

When the favor of God resides on your life it is almost as if the "rules" don't apply to you. I am not by any means saying you can just go around and break the rules, what I am saying is that you become the exception to the rule.

For example, there may be a company with a policy that they say no one can get around, and the next thing you know here you are around this unshakable policy. Or in my experience I have gotten jobs I have not even applied for, that people were lined up to apply for. A lot of people don't like to discuss favor because it is not extended to just anyone, there are qualifications to get to the land of favor, and everybody wants it but not everyone wants to go through the process to get it. And though it is obtainable, one must live a holy lifestyle to "truly" walk in God's favor and not everyone is willing to live a compromise free life. Yes there may be times when you experience Gods favor, but to truly live a favored life makes you feel like you are on God's "priority list!"

Yes favor is a very "touch subject" because no one wants to hear you say that you are favored especially when they feel as though they are not. It is ok to embrace the favor of God on your life because like your anointing, it cost you something Just like that strong aroma that is smelled when someone first enters a room, when you are favored or in the presence of favor, you can just tell. The atmosphere is going to change. You may as well wear a sign or nametag because everyone around you seems to be able to tell. But just as good as it smells to those around you, it tastes even better in your mouth. Once you have continuously experienced it there is nothing else that you would rather have. God does give "preferential treatment" to his children and we do not have to be ashamed to be favored by God! Yes we will get some things people will say we do not deserve and they are right. Yes we will walk through doors, that should have been closed, and yes we will become the exception to the rule! O well! Lift up your head, and walk right into the prepared places God has for you. And when people get upset at you because of your special treatment just smile as you shrug your shoulders and say, "God favors me!" In the words of my sister and former pastor, Dr. Cynthia Wolford "favor ain't fair, but it sure is fabulous!" Be blessed favored people of God!

Psalm 41:11 (KJV)
*By this I know that thou **favour**est me, because mine enemy doth not triumph over me.*

Pour out Your Spirit

Pour out your spirit on your people
Saturate the atmosphere (ooooh)
We're in need of a visitation from you
Don't let us leave here the same way we came
Please pour out your spirit in this place

Pour out (3xs)
Shower down your anointing (healing, blessing, love, peace)

Don't let us leave here the same way we came
Please pour out your spirit in this place

With Arms Stretched High

With arms stretched high, I surrender all
All to your will all to your way
Forgive me Lord I want to be changed
Take my will conform it to yours
I surrender all with arms stretched high

Take my will conform it to yours (repeat)
I surrender all (3xs)
With arms stretched high

Transition into hymn—"I Surrender All"

Be Fruitful

Lead

In the beginning we were told to be fruitful and multiply
Life was not the only thing God meant by that reply
Not all trees were for our eating, though it had plenty to share
And you will know the tree by the fruit in which bears

Chorus

The fruit is love, and joy, and peace
Patience kindness goodness and faithfulness
We must show gentleness and self control
Be ye fruitful and multiply

Lead

A new commandment I give unto you
That you love one another, the way that I love you
By this all men will know that are my disciple
If you love

Chorus

The fruit is love, and joy, and peace
Patience kindness goodness and faithfulness
We must show gentleness and self control
Be ye fruitful and multiply
Be ye fruitful and multiply

Lead

Be full of the fruit of spirit-And reproduce it

Be-e-e-e-e-e-e-e-e Fruitful

Be-e-e-e-e-e-e—e-e-e-e

Be-e-e-e-e-e-e-e-e Fruitful

Be full of the fruit of spirit-And reproduce it

Be ye fruitful

Be ye fruitful oh

Be ye fruitful

Fruitful oh

Be ye fruitful and multiply

A Psalmist's Prayer

Lead

Our Father, which art in heaven, grant me serenity
Thy Kingdom come, Thy will be done on earth, but do it
through me

Chorus

This is a prayer of a psalmist
And earnest prayer from the soul of the redeemed
This is a prayer from your servant
Whose heart has been freed

Lead

Give me this day my daily bread, and forgive me for all of
my sins
Lead me not into temptation, but deliver me from evil
hands

Chorus

This is a prayer of a psalmist
And earnest prayer from the soul of the redeemed
This is a prayer from your servant
Whose heart has been freed

Declaration

For thine is the kingdom and the power and the glory
forever and ever
Amen

You Are God

Verse one

You are joy you are peace you are creator of all things
You are love you are truth my life it is the proof
You are the lily in the valley the bright and morning star
That's who you are, you are God

Chorus

You are God, and besides you there is no other
You are God and you reign eternally
One day every knee, shall bow, and every tongue confess
that you are God!
You are God!

Verse two

You are word you are spirit you are the reason for our
being
You're resurrection you are life, the only way to you is
Christ
You are alpha and omega, the beginning and the end
That's who you are, you are God

Chorus

You are God, and besides you there is no other
You are God and you reign eternally
One day every knee, shall bow, and every tongue confess
that you are God!
You are God!

Vamp

Altos: You are God-4xs
Tenors: There is no other you are God
Sopranos: And you reign eternally
You are God! You are God! You are God!

I'm Sorry

An interlude Written by, Patience "PJ" Ivy
Arranged by LaMeshia Shaw-Tanimowo

Chorus
Lord I'm sorry, I'm sorray, I'm sorray

Verse: Lord I know I've done some unpleasing things to thee. And that's why I say Lord I'm sorray.

Chorus
Lord I'm sorry, I'm sorray, I'm sorray

Verse
Lord please forgive me for those unpleasing things. Please accept my apology.

Chorus
Lord I'm sorry, I'm sorray, I'm sorray

All
Lord I am so sorray!

Strength

When you think of the word "strength" there are several things that may come to your mind. You may think of someone who is physically built, with rippling triceps and biceps and a six pack. You may think of someone athletic like a wrestler or a boxer, with iron calves and thighs. Perhaps you may consider someone who moves things around or who works out and can lift large amounts of weight. Maybe you consider your mother to be strong in spirit because of what she endured during labor and all the sacrifices she made to provide for you. Or you may consider a soldier or someone who is battling a life threatening disease to be the ones who possess strength. All of these things and many others are very common thoughts when the words "strength" or "strong" are spoken and all of them are correct. I believe that it is ok for everyone to have their own definition of strength.

People who really know me know that I have a bubbling personality. I love to joke and kid around. I love to laugh and make other people laugh. It is just something about a laugh, a grin, a smirk or a smile, that really changes the inner mood of people. It is as if it's a temporary escape from everything that is going on in their lives. For that brief second it's a passage of freedom into a world that does not normally exist for them. I am often told that "I missed my calling!" I have heard that numerous times from friends, family, co-workers, and perfect strangers as well. They always tell me "girl you are crazy, you should be a comedian!" I usually laugh it off and say something sarcastic that starts them to laughing all over again. I learned that I am most funny to people when I am being serious, when I am not trying to crack a joke at all.

There is one mother at my church, whom I adore. She is short in stature and is always dressed to the "T!" She is a little woman but boy is she full of power. There is definitely an anointing on her life and you can tell the moment you come in contact with her. One day I got an unexpected call from her. She told me that she was working on the staff for our church Christmas party and that they wanted to know if I would be interested in being on program. I immediately said yes because I thought she was asking me to sing, and that is something that I know I am gifted by God to do and something that I love to do as it is therapy for me. She quickly informed me that it was not to sing that they wanted something different. Well I was confused, I thought what could they want me to do? Well whatever it was I was ready to say "yes" until she dropped the bomb on me. She said that she wanted me to do about ten to fifteen minutes of comedy. "What?" I said and she immediately began to laugh. "Uh I have to think about that one!" But she quickly assured me that I would do a great job, and how I always make people laugh, her in particular and she loved it. It was not as if this was the first time I had ever heard this, but it was the first time anyone had ever challenged me, or offered me a chance to do anything other than just sing since I had been in Georgia! She was always so kind and I really did appreciate the offer, so I said yes, even though I was scared to death.

I had no idea at all what I would say. There is a difference between clowning around and having to have a structured list of jokes. I have so much respect for comedians. It's hard when people know that you are supposed to make them laugh. It is as if they try their hardest not to laugh just because they know that's your job. Yet I had agreed to do it, and I am a woman of my word, plus there was just no way I could let mother down. I showed up at the party nervous as can be! None of my family or church members knew why I was so nervous, as I had been instructed not to tell anyone because I was a "surprise guest." I had practiced and rehearsed what I was going to say and how I was going to say it and I was ready. But when I got up there everything I had practiced went out of the window. I could remember a few of my jokes, and the crowd seemed to be enjoying it. However I had some great material I never got to because my nerves kicked in and I didn't have one single note card on stage with me. So I winged it! I just did what I knew how to do. Make myself laugh. Those were probably the longest fifteen minutes of my life. But when I was done everyone was laughing and clapping and I felt good about it. I don't know if they were just being polite because we were in a church setting, but it didn't matter to me! I felt awesome.

I often think about that moment. I was so grateful to God that he had laid it on mother's heart to have me walk in a different light than everyone was use to seeing me in. Sometime when you are good at one thing, you get trapped there because people know you do it, and do it well and often times never ask you of your other gifts, talents, aspirations, or anointings, nor do they always try to find out what else you can do. I will never forget the day she called me. I cried and cried and cried. They were tears of joy. Little did she know I had been going through a very difficult time in my life and though I put on a good show on the outside, on the inside I was all messed up. There were some decisions I was battling with, some disappointments and delays I was trying to overcome, and all week long I had been in a "funk." And this assignment gave me no choice but to smile. I wondered if God had told mother my secret, that I wasn't always so bubbly and happy because I wanted to be, but because that was one of the ways I gained strength to move on.

Sometimes people have preconceived notions about you. They assume you are just silly and or immature because you are always joking and laughing. They think that you don't take life seriously or that you couldn't possibly have a serious and close relationship with God. But they don't know how many nights I cried myself to sleep dealing with the hurts and the pains that this world is known to bring. They have no clue of the many hours I laid prostate before God and stayed on my knees praying. They have no clue about all the fasting and praying I did because I didn't walk around announcing that I was on a fast. Because I learned that what I needed only God could provide. They did not know of all the songs I had composed to encourage myself, all the poems I had written to release my pain and bring in but a bit of sunshine. They were unaware of all the days I had to drag myself out of bed to do what came naturally to the rest of the world, and I wore a face that said I had it all together, although I was just about ready to throw in the towel. Thankfully God had already "delivered me from people." Meaning what people thought and said didn't matter to me anymore, as that use to be one of the things I had the hardest time dealing with.

It often puzzled me how Christians would walk around quoting scriptures and clichés about joy but had no real joy of their own. "Joy comes in the morning" they would say, and to myself I would think "I can't wait 'til they wake up!" or this is one of my favorites, "this joy that I have the world didn't give it to me and the world can't take it away!" . . . and the world don't want it, uh what joy? I have never even seen you smile. If you cracked one right now dust would probably fly from the corners of your mouth because they haven't turned up in so long, I thought. I wanted to know why we as Christians, proclaimed so much joy and happiness yet seemed so uptight and at the person who oozed with joy that we could see, we get so disgusted by them. Life has taught me that not everyone knows what it was like to have the absence of joy! Because if they did, when they came in contact with joy again they would be oozing too!

I have had my share of trials just like everyone else. But there was something God had really given me that made it possible for me to keep on going. One of my favorite scriptures is Nehemiah 8:10b and it describes it best.

*"10 And Nehemiah continued, "Go and celebrate with a feast of rich foods and sweet drinks, and share gifts of food with people who have nothing prepared. This is a sacred day before our Lord. Don't be dejected and sad, **for the joy of the** LORD **is your strength!**" (New Living Translation)*

That scripture is so real to me. The joy that God had given me really had been my strength. I laughed and cracked jokes about life because, had I thought another moment about what was actually going on I would have taken my own life, just to escape from the pain that I was feeling. God gave me joy as my way of getting a taste a freedom just when I needed it, and it always seemed to help, even if the feeling was temporary at one point. Although mother probably didn't have a clue of what I was going through, God once again sent the remedy to my problem, the prescription for my sadness and this time through the hands of mother. That call was a simple reminder that I have a reason to smile, laugh, and even crack Jokes. That the God who lives on the inside of me, has given me a precious gift of joy and it is not supposed to be a hidden treasure. I was reminded that I actually draw strength from the joy of the Lord, and that is nothing to be ashamed of. I bless God that I know what it is like to have no joy at all, because now I appreciate the joy he has given to me. Now I don't wrestle with how people conceive my joy and I don't make excuses for it either. God has restored the wounded areas of my life and replaced them with a joy that is so unspeakable. Just writing this has me oozing with gladness.

Strength can be defined in so many ways and again I believe everyone has the right to their own definition of strength. But as for me I completely agree with Nehemiah and my life is the evidence that a little joy will take you a long way, and that God has already placed strength down inside you and that is his joy. It's the Joy of the Lord that should stand out more than any tricep, bicep, six pack, or any other muscle. Its Gods great joy that we shouldn't be ashamed to show off and expose the world too. It is the power that God has given us to illuminate this dark world. I encourage you to allow the Joy of the Lord to strengthen the weak areas in your life. To boldly be able to stand and declare to the enemy that every trap that he sets doesn't break or destroy you, it just adds weight to your spiritual dumbbells and the more you allow "*God's Joy*" to reign the stronger you get and are able to lift those roadblocks right out of your way. So let's get physically fit in the spirit. Crack a smile, laugh at a joke, and tell a joke of your own. Consider this your alarm clock, it's now morning and joy is here, posses it and be strengthened!

Psalm 5:11-12(NIV)

[11] *But let all who take refuge in you be glad; let them ever sing for joy. Spread your protection over them that those who love your name may rejoice in you.*
[12] *Surely, Lord, you bless the righteous; you surround them with your favor as with a shield.*

~10 of My Favorite Psalms from the Bible~

Psalms 1

King James Version (KJV)

Blessed is the man that walketh not in the counsel of the ungodly, nor standeth in the way of sinners, nor sitteth in the seat of the scornful.

² But his delight is in the law of the LORD; and in his law doth he meditate day and night.

³ And he shall be like a tree planted by the rivers of water, that bringeth forth his fruit in his season; his leaf also shall not wither; and whatsoever he doeth shall prosper.

⁴ The ungodly are not so: but are like the chaff which the wind driveth away.

⁵ Therefore the ungodly shall not stand in the judgment, nor sinners in the congregation of the righteous.

⁶ For the LORD knoweth the way of the righteous: but the way of the ungodly shall perish.

Psalms 19

King James Version (KJV)

The heavens declare the glory of God; and the firmament sheweth his handywork.

² Day unto day uttereth speech, and night unto night sheweth knowledge.

³ There is no speech nor language, where their voice is not heard.

⁴ Their line is gone out through all the earth, and their words to the end of the world. In them hath he set a tabernacle for the sun,

⁵ Which is as a bridegroom coming out of his chamber, and rejoiceth as a strong man to run a race.

⁶ His going forth is from the end of the heaven, and his circuit unto the ends of it: and there is nothing hid from the heat thereof.

⁷ The law of the LORD is perfect, converting the soul: the testimony of the LORD is sure, making wise the simple.

⁸ The statutes of the LORD are right, rejoicing the heart: the commandment of the LORD is pure, enlightening the eyes.

⁹ The fear of the LORD is clean, enduring for ever: the judgments of the LORD are true and righteous altogether.

¹⁰ More to be desired are they than gold, yea, than much fine gold: sweeter also than honey and the honeycomb.

¹¹ Moreover by them is thy servant warned: and in keeping of them there is great reward.

¹² Who can understand his errors? cleanse thou me from secret faults.

¹³ Keep back thy servant also from presumptuous sins; let them not have dominion over me: then shall I be upright, and I shall be innocent from the great transgression.

¹⁴ Let the words of my mouth, and the meditation of my heart, be acceptable in thy sight, O LORD, my strength, and my redeemer.

Psalms 23

King James Version (KJV)

The LORD is my shepherd; I shall not want.

2 He maketh me to lie down in green pastures: he leadeth me beside the still waters.

3 He restoreth my soul: he leadeth me in the paths of righteousness for his name's sake.

4 Yea, though I walk through the valley of the shadow of death, I will fear no evil: for thou art with me; thy rod and thy staff they comfort me.

5 Thou preparest a table before me in the presence of mine enemies: thou anointest my head with oil; my cup runneth over.

6 Surely goodness and mercy shall follow me all the days of my life: and I will dwell in the house of the LORD forever.

Psalms 24

King James Version (KJV)

T he earth is the Lord's, and the fullness thereof; the world, and they that dwell therein.

² For he hath founded it upon the seas, and established it upon the floods.

³ Who shall ascend into the hill of the Lord? or who shall stand in his holy place?

⁴ He that hath clean hands, and a pure heart; who hath not lifted up his soul unto vanity, nor sworn deceitfully.

⁵ He shall receive the blessing from the Lord, and righteousness from the God of his salvation.

⁶ This is the generation of them that seek him, that seek thy face, O Jacob. Selah.

⁷ Lift up your heads, O ye gates; and be ye lift up, ye everlasting doors; and the King of glory shall come in.

⁸ Who is this King of glory? The Lord strong and mighty, theLord mighty in battle.

⁹ Lift up your heads, O ye gates; even lift them up, ye everlasting doors; and the King of glory shall come in.
¹⁰ Who is this King of glory? The Lord of hosts, he is the King of glory. Selah.

Psalms 27

King James Version (KJV)

The LORD is my light and my salvation; whom shall I fear? The LORD is the strength of my life; of whom shall I be afraid?

² When the wicked, even mine enemies and my foes, came upon me to eat up my flesh, they stumbled and fell.

³ Though an host should encamp against me, my heart shall not fear: though war should rise against me, in this will I be confident.

⁴ One thing have I desired of the LORD, that will I seek after; that I may dwell in the house of the LORD all the days of my life, to behold the beauty of the LORD, and to enquire in his temple.

⁵ For in the time of trouble he shall hide me in his pavilion: in the secret of his tabernacle shall he hide me; he shall set me up upon a rock.

⁶ And now shall mine head be lifted up above mine enemies round about me: therefore will I offer in his tabernacle sacrifices of joy; I will sing, yea, I will sing praises unto the LORD.

[7] Hear, O Lord, when I cry with my voice: have mercy also upon me, and answer me.

[8] When thou saidst, Seek ye my face; my heart said unto thee, Thy face, Lord, will I seek.

[9] Hide not thy face far from me; put not thy servant away in anger: thou hast been my help; leave me not, neither forsake me, O God of my salvation.

[10] When my father and my mother forsake me, then the Lord will take me up.

[11] Teach me thy way, O Lord, and lead me in a plain path, because of mine enemies.

[12] Deliver me not over unto the will of mine enemies: for false witnesses are risen up against me, and such as breathe out cruelty.

[13] I had fainted, unless I had believed to see the goodness of the Lord in the land of the living.

[14] Wait on the Lord: be of good courage, and he shall strengthen thine heart: wait, I say, on the Lord.

Psalms 46

King James Version (KJV)

God is our refuge and strength, a very present help in trouble.

² Therefore will not we fear, though the earth be removed, and though the mountains be carried into the midst of the sea;

³ Though the waters thereof roar and be troubled, though the mountains shake with the swelling thereof. Selah.

⁴ There is a river, the streams whereof shall make glad the city of God, the holy place of the tabernacles of the most High.

⁵ God is in the midst of her; she shall not be moved: God shall help her, and that right early.

⁶ The heathen raged, the kingdoms were moved: he uttered his voice, the earth melted.

⁷ The Lord of hosts is with us; the God of Jacob is our refuge. Selah.

⁸ Come, behold the works of the Lord, what desolations he hath made in the earth.

⁹ He maketh wars to cease unto the end of the earth; he breaketh the bow, and cutteth the spear in sunder; he burneth the chariot in the fire.

¹⁰ Be still, and know that I am God: I will be exalted among the heathen, I will be exalted in the earth.

¹¹ The Lord of hosts is with us; the God of Jacob is our refuge. Selah.

Psalms 91

King James Version (KJV)

He that dwelleth in the secret place of the most High shall abide under the shadow of the Almighty.

² I will say of the LORD, He is my refuge and my fortress: my God; in him will I trust.

³ Surely he shall deliver thee from the snare of the fowler, and from the noisome pestilence.

⁴ He shall cover thee with his feathers, and under his wings shalt thou trust: his truth shall be thy shield and buckler.

⁵ Thou shalt not be afraid for the terror by night; nor for the arrow that flieth by day;

⁶ Nor for the pestilence that walketh in darkness; nor for the destruction that wasteth at noonday.

⁷ A thousand shall fall at thy side, and ten thousand at thy right hand; but it shall not come nigh thee.

⁸ Only with thine eyes shalt thou behold and see the reward of the wicked.

[9] Because thou hast made the LORD, which is my refuge, even the most High, thy habitation;

[10] There shall no evil befall thee, neither shall any plague come nigh thy dwelling.

[11] For he shall give his angels charge over thee, to keep thee in all thy ways.

[12] They shall bear thee up in their hands, lest thou dash thy foot against a stone.

[13] Thou shalt tread upon the lion and adder: the young lion and the dragon shalt thou trample under feet.

[14] Because he hath set his love upon me, therefore will I deliver him: I will set him on high, because he hath known my name.

[15] He shall call upon me, and I will answer him: I will be with him in trouble; I will deliver him, and honour him.

[16] With long life will I satisfy him, and shew him my salvation.

Psalms 100

King James Version (KJV)

Make a joyful noise unto the Lord, all ye lands.

² Serve the Lord with gladness: come before his presence with singing.

³ Know ye that the Lord he is God: it is he that hath made us, and not we ourselves; we are his people, and the sheep of his pasture.

⁴ Enter into his gates with thanksgiving, and into his courts with praise: be thankful unto him, and bless his name.

⁵ For the Lord is good; his mercy is everlasting; and his truth endureth to all generations.

Psalms 121

King James Version (KJV)

I will lift up mine eyes unto the hills, from whence cometh my help.

² My help cometh from the LORD, which made heaven and earth.

³ He will not suffer thy foot to be moved: he that keepeth thee will not slumber.

⁴ Behold, he that keepeth Israel shall neither slumber nor sleep.

⁵ The LORD is thy keeper: the LORD is thy shade upon thy right hand.

⁶ The sun shall not smite thee by day, nor the moon by night.

⁷ The LORD shall preserve thee from all evil: he shall preserve thy soul.

⁸ The LORD shall preserve thy going out and thy coming in from this time forth, and even for evermore.

Psalms 150

King James Version (KJV)

Praise ye the Lord. Praise God in his sanctuary: praise him in the firmament of his power.

² Praise him for his mighty acts: praise him according to his excellent greatness.

³ Praise him with the sound of the trumpet: praise him with the psaltery and harp.

⁴ Praise him with the timbrel and dance: praise him with stringed instruments and organs.

⁵ Praise him upon the loud cymbals: praise him upon the high sounding cymbals.

⁶ Let everything that hath breath praise the Lord. Praise ye the Lord.

Stir up the Gift

What do you want to be when you grow up? I can remember that question being asked so many times when I was a little girl. It seemed like every adult I knew would ask me that question. I would always have a great response. "I want to be a writer, a singer, an actress a television star, a lawyer, and an entrepreneur." Over the years my answer had changed to a more professional response. The older I got the more career oriented I got, because I would hear things like ok that's great but which one of those do you want to be? Or if that doesn't work out what will you do? Although I secretly still desired to do all of those things I would only say aloud the professional ones like lawyer, psychologist social worker or entrepreneur. None of these answers were lies. I actually at one time or another in my life was either extremely interested in these careers or had even studied or worked in those capacities.

There is something precious and special about a child with a dream. When we are young we are fired up and excited about our future because we can visualize ourselves doing that thing we want to do and being great at it. And even at that age we will start working on it. My older cousin Hope was my first unofficial "Manager." And she didn't just manage me, all the little cousins, were under her management. She wrote the songs, recorded them on cassette and we had to perform them and be very serious about it. One Time we even made a music video, and because there was no rain outside and the song called for a rainy scene, she taught us creativity by sending us outside with a water hose to spray on the window of the house, to give the illusion that it was raining. It was brilliant, just to come back in sit down and watch and listen to what we had created was amazing. We always had such a great time, and I knew I could do this full time. I felt like I could cross singer and television star off my "dreams to do list."

Antoinette is another one of my first cousins and we use to spend the night over one another's house quite frequently. The thing to do was to go to summer camp at the neighborhood park by day and skating on a basketball court of that same park by night. We had our summer planned out and the only thing that was stopping us was money, or so she thought. My mom was a firm believer that you never go to anyone's house empty handed. So when I would go stay she often sent snacks and treats for us. You know juices, whole pickles, candy, chips, freeze pops and etc. Well the entrepreneur in me said, "Problem solved!" I told Antoinette that when her mom, my Aunt LaTonya goes to work, all we had to do was take a table outside, create some signs and sell every snack we could get our hands on. She was hesitant at first but she finally complied and the sell was on! The plan was fool proof, everything went exactly as planned and as a matter of fact we never got caught. See even at eight and nine I understood inventory control and supply and demand. It wasn't until we were about twenty-nine that we shared with our parents how we were able to maintain skating money. The funny thing is that they thought it was free all along. Entrepreneur, check!

Now there was Marcus, Aaron, and Shena, which were probably my closest friends ever. We are actually all first cousins, but were raised more like brother and sister. We were always together and at a few times in life we even lived together. We went to the same schools were involved in the same community activities and we never had a dull moment. There were actually a ton of us first cousins that were about the same age, there was also; Michael, Deron, DeAngelo, Mook, Keandra, and just so many more of us (all of us under Hope's Management). But the four of us were inseparable. We did things that even now that we are adults I cannot disclose, because our mother's and our grandparents would go crazy. Marcus was the eldest of the four of us, so we pretty much did everything he said, and he knew it! We got into plenty mischief, but it seemed to be so adventurous, and so fun that we didn't mind doing it again. Daily Shena and I would come home with bruises, scrapes and knots from trying to be one of the boys. She was much more dare-devilish than I. Anyway I don't know who found out about it first but there was a candy van that drove kids around and allowed them to sell candy, and if you actually sold something, you got a percentage in cash that day. The catch was you had to be eleven and Aaron, Shena, and myself, who are only days apart were all under age. Long story short we talked to the man and it was too good of a deal to pass up so we lied about our age, ran the permission slip home and off to work we went! Nine years old with my first job. Life was great the job was easy, all we had to do is give some speech about being a part of the "Kansas Kid" program which was designed to keep kids off the street, and try to sell saltwater taffy at a ridiculous price that we often even changed for greater profit (shhh! That part was a secret) and then meet him back at the corner and ride to the next street. We were nine but we were rich. We made loads of cash and couldn't wait until he came and picked us up. Before he would take us home we usually stopped by Taco Tico or a gas station so we could load up on stuff we didn't need anyway, mostly candy and junk food. O how I loved that job and I probably would have retired from there (smile), if it had not been for my Aunt Rosa, Marcus and Aaron's mom who got all of us including the neighborhood kids fired, because she threatened bodily harm and cursed out our boss because she accused him of being a child molester for driving a load of kids around in a creepy "Scooby-Doo" looking van. Needless to say he never came back to pick us up however, for a short while I had been quite the business woman.

I have been writing since I was a little girl. As far back as I can remember I have had an imagination that I wanted to put down on paper. My Best friend Bianca and I would hang out a lot and we loved doing stuff. We wanted to be everywhere and do everything, like any other kid I suppose. We wouldn't play with dolls or makeup. You could usually find us outside bike riding, walking, or dancing. And if you did not find us outside, we were surely inside writing stories, creating characters and planning on doing this is a lifelong career. Yes at a young age we had it all figured out. She was quite artistic. She could draw people who actually looked like people, unlike my pictures which usually turned into a guessing game of what is that? She could draw their clothes and houses and everything. We both would write create a whole story filled with dramatic details and characters whose personality came to life within minutes. We use to say that one day we would work together, that I would be the writer and actress and she would be the director and producer. It was a great plan we thought, and we took it seriously. By the age of eleven we had notebooks full of stories, poems, plays, movie scripts, songs, and anything else that could be written.

As we grew older we never stopped writing. However our dreams and goals were beginning to change. We decided to pursue careers in Business administration and business management. And as life would have it, we had a dry season of not pursuing the big dream, at least not together anyway. Life seemed to constantly remind me that there were more important things to do than write such as; get a degree, find a well paying job with great benefits, pay the bills, get married, and prepare for a prosperous future. So I did all of those things, and they were rewarding, but there is nothing like doing what you love to do. No matter what I did I would always have a notebook with me, I would always use my family and friends as my audience to "critique" my writings, and creative ideas.

When God first told me to write a book I was pumped up and super excited, I had writing time scheduled into my day and I couldn't be happier. What an accomplishment being an author would be. After all, throughout my schooling all of my English and language arts teachers praised my writings and creativity, this was a great idea. Then I began writing what I thought would be my first book. I had been through some things in life and I knew that if I shared them, they would surely bless others. I wrote for over a year and would tell everyone "I'm writing a book!" Every time I thought the book was finished something else would happen that I felt should be included. It happen so often I started naming events in my life by the chapter. Something would happen and I would sigh and say "chapter 13," another crisis would occur and again I would sigh and say "chapter 14' and this went on and on. I thought how can I ever release this book, if I can't seem to get to the happy ending? Then God revealed this book was not finished so I needed to move to another book.

This was exciting because I would be able to write a juicy novel and maybe somebody would love it so much that it would become a motion picture or at least a *Lifetime* movie! So I also started that book and I was excited again. Long story short it wasn't time for those books either. I have always loved poetry and I wrote it often, more as therapy for me, or for special occasions. This was too personal I did not want to share my poems, because, "what if people didn't like them, what if people could tell there was no technique and that I basically just wrote how I felt and called it poetry? So many excuses ran through me. Yet again I begin to pick through some poems and songs I had written, and begin to right a few more. I had paid for the self publishing package in full, and really had enough poetry just to submit, yet again something was telling me that it wasn't good enough and that I should put it off. This went on for three years! Finally I had a complete book that God had given me the ok to release and I did not want to release it. On the outside I would still talk about it and tell people it was coming out but there was this fear of failure that hovered over me like a dark cloud in a stormy sky, although I had always loved to write and I desired to release books, and everything else in life I said I would do I just did and without pause. This was one thing really had me stuck.

There are different types of writing styles and different formats and categories of poetry, there is haiku, allegory, lyrical, verse, imagery, irony, and the list goes on and on. The fear is that because I have never been formally trained in these techniques, the critics would eat me alive! I finally had enough of the running and decided this is something I wanted to do for myself. This was a lifelong dream and even if I just published it that would be success enough for me. That I didn't have to be able to be put in a category, that I could still write my novel and my life coaching book and still release my thoughts on the different times in my life and the pain and suffering I felt and how God allowed me to overcome it. Some of my poems are just general poems and may seem that there is nothing profound about them at all, either way I refused to allow the fear of failure to rule anymore. Releasing this book was for me, so here we are three years later from when I originally started writing this book and I am excited about it. I may not have written anything in this book in its "proper" format. But what I do know is when I write, I feel great. It's a release for me, and other people seem to enjoy it and be blessed by it whether it makes them laugh, cry, challenges them to pursue a dream, or just bring back memories. I had to obey God and fulfill my lifelong dream or becoming a published author and poet.

I am so glad I had such supportive parents, family members and close friends who embraced everything I did. They made me do whatever I decided to do to the best of my ability, with a standard of excellence. They encouraged me, gave me real criticism and feedback, and was just such a blessing. This section was never meant to go into the actual book. It was more as a thank you letter to those who had stood beside me for so long, but there is something about being transparent that helps heal others around you. There may be someone reading this or someone you know that really needs to know that it is not too late to fulfill your dreams and that even if you have never received the proper training in the craft in which you love, that you have to overcome the fear of failure and discouragement and go forth anyway, because "someone is waiting for you to do you so that they can be blessed!"

Parents, teachers, pastors, siblings, neighbors and friends, be an encourager. Support the people in your community. Buy a dinner at their restaurant or function, order one of their homemade cakes, purchase their cd or book, show up at their concerts, plays or recitals, help them pass out flyers, speak a kind word to them that gives them the strength to go on, or do whatever you can do to persuade them to chase their dreams. Help stir up the gifts that are inside of them, if you have the expertise and or training in that area share what you know. Never be afraid to impart life into someone. The world can change one dream at a time, and you can help. It is ok to have several dreams, and believe it or not, they can all be fulfilled. Never poison people with words of discouragement or with dream killing tactics like laughing at them when they share their dreams and inventions, saying that the idea is stupid or will never work, or that you can't believe they are the ones who want to complete the task.

Think about your favorite dish that your mother makes or grandmother made. You may have tasted that dish many times by many different people, but it just didn't taste like grandma's version, something was missing. Dreams are like soup, there are so many components to it. Maybe there is more than one thing you desire from life. Perhaps you want to be a mother, a college graduate, a dancer, and a business owner. Well all of those ingredients dumped together in one pot do not look appetizing. However once you add water (your actions), a little seasoning (your creativity), some fire (a little discouragement, or frustration of things not going your way) there is an aroma that is created, a flavor that the world has been waiting to taste. Once that scent is released you will get a few pot stirrers (supporters, people who encourage you. Understand sometimes you may have to be your own stirrer). Some will last only a moment and the others will be there until the end. However your stirrers cannot stir what does not exist! Just like grandma's sweet potato pie and mama's Mac & cheese, others have come along with their own versions of those recipes. In other words, yes there are a lot of authors already, sure there are many great singers and dancers. Yet there is something about their recipe that just doesn't taste right. There is something that is missing and that something is you!

2 Timothy 1:6-7 KJV

"Wherefore I put thee in remembrance that thou stir up the gift of God, which is in thee by putting on of my hands. For God hath not given us the spirit of fear; but of power, and of love, and of a sound mind."

I love this scripture because it reminds me that we are to stir up the gift that God has placed inside of us and that He did not give us the spirit of fear. So whatever it is that you know you should be doing and just have not stepped out into. I hope this book has enticed you to complete the dream that is inside of you. I stand as one of your stirrers (your encourager), and I want to make sure you know that all things are possible. It is not too late and yes you are the right one for the job! We are waiting on your soup to be completed, don't just be a pot of stuff! Stand up and send off the aroma of you! This is your time! Your gifts, your dreams, and/or your desires are not dead, STIR THEM UP!

~QUOTES AND NOTES~

Quotes

"*I am who I am, nothing more, nothing less. I have to be me, because me is who I know best.*"

"*Be inspired, be empowered, be blessed.*"

"*If I am going to do the same thing today, that I did yesterday, what is the purpose for tomorrow? Because soon tomorrow will be today, and today will be yesterday, and I would have spent them all the same.*"

"*Dream-Plan-Be!*"

"*Who or what defines success? Does your financial status, social groups, degrees and accolades? Or is succeeding, the mere accomplishment of that in which you envisioned that you would complete in your own mind?*"

"*Don't be afraid to try, be afraid not to.*"

"*You have the power to possess all of your hearts desires. You must first seek, reach, and keep. Often times we have already had what we desire, but we let it slip away. Because in order to possess we must get rid of our mess. And that seems to be much more difficult than obtaining that which we think we cannot live without.*"

"Wear a smile, it looks good on you!"

"I cannot be a singer without first learning a note. I cannot be a poet if I only read what you wrote. I cannot profess to be a writer and not even own a pen. I cannot be a dreamer if I cannot see the end."

"Stand tall-Look forward-Press forth!"

Quotes

"Big are your dreams—mighty are your actions. You can never fail if you put your dreams into actions, because together they are big and mighty."

"Praise is the appetizer for worship. It is the snack before the main course!"

"People who discourage you from achieving your dreams are like armed robbers, because they snatch what is most valuable to you, and secretly run off and try and produce it themselves."

"Creativity is a weapon that allows you to conquer your circumstances."

"When others count you out, count on God!"

"If someone made a list of all the lives you've touched, how long would your credits be?"

"Your schemes can't kill my dreams."

"If someone wanted to make a film about your life, what would they celebrate and remember?"

"Praise is the beautiful scenery on your journey, and worship is your destination."

"Whatever you do today make sure it takes you a step closer to your destiny!"

Quotes

"Maturity is not measured by the number of years you have lived. It's measured by the wisdom you have acquired and how you use that wisdom in life's situations!"

"SHOUT! Sing Hallelujah Out loud Until Triumph comes!"

"We have all experienced things in our life that have detoured us on our journey to our destiny. However it is up to you alone, whether you allow those situations to pause or paralyze you!"

"Created in His image designed to give Him praise!"

"Today is a new day. Yesterday is gone, tomorrow is not promised, and the rest of your day is not guaranteed. So forgive yourself for yesterday, make preparations for tomorrow, but live and love today!"

"If you want to make it to the top, you must see yourself there first."

"You should be number one on your fan list. No one should support your dreams, goals, and talents more than you."

"Failure is the absence of persistence!"

"Surround yourself with like-minded individuals who refuse to give up. Their perseverance will push you to possess your purpose."

"The ability to think is the presence of freedom."

Quotes

"Time is more valuable than any precious stone or jewel because it cannot be replaced. You get one chance to see it, one chance to use it, one chance to make it shine!"

"Laughter is the song of the soul!"

"Declare war on your enemies, by doing what they say you will never get done!"

"Let your hands and feet move more than your mouth!"

"If you subtracted your bad deeds from your good deeds, what would the outcome be?"

"Beauty is believing you are more than what the evidence presents!"

"Perform CPR on your dreams and ideas, and revive the things in your life that you allowed to die before their time."

"Allow your character to speak louder than the controversy concerning you."

"Ignite the fire of your aspirations again by sparking interest in the things that once fueled you."

"Instead of trying to impress others, convince yourself!"

Notes

- All poems, songs, inspirational readings, and quotes are original, written by LaMeshia Shaw-Tanimowo except "I'm Sorry" written by Patience Ivy, used with permission.
- Patience Ivy is the younger sister of LaMeshia Shaw-Tanimowo and she wrote the song "I'm Sorry," when she was only 11 years old!
- The song "Divine Purpose" was written by LaMeshia Shaw-Tanimowo in 2006 as a title track for the gospel duo group she co-founded with her first cousin Porsche Harris under the same name. This song has been recorded and performed by the group on many occasions including when they were one of the opening acts for gospel recording artist Vashawn Mitchell in Beloit, Wisconsin in 2006 and Grammy award winner Pastor Hezekiah Walker in Augusta Georgia in 2007!
- The song "Sho Nuf" was written by LaMeshia Shaw-Tanimowo at the age of 16!
- The poem "Heaven Called Your Name" was written by LaMeshia Shaw-Tanimowo in the year 2000 after the death of her aunt. This poem was printed in the obituary.
- The photo of the sunset, located by the poem "W.O.W" was photographed by LaMeshia Shaw-Tanimowo in Georgia.

www.somelodic.com

*For booking and calendar information or to purchase a copy
of this book, other merchandise, and future books please visit
www.somelodic.com or www.facebook.com/melodicme*